The Life and Times of
EDWARD II

Princeps Edwarde, non tua lancea tarde
In Scotos mota, p[er] te dic Cambria nota.

En temps doneyt moy suffyseint damurge fortune si
Deuer mest fayle, q[ue] estoit mon age bien souent
El mound nad si bel, ne si sage, ou autres ne p...
Si euer ne lui coupt damurge, q[ue]l ne serra ...
A damoury fays moy prens naturgit d cele en qi ...
De cheo a[n] cost estent ne me deueys[e] trop affier
Les g[ra]ndes hous qe fest a ment qe Jeo me ... quey en
... ou amer e mettis plaint en fort ...son me ...
... me s[on]t eurelement ... ne ... sey ...

The Life and Times of

EDWARD II

Caroline Bingham

Introduction by Antonia Fraser

Book Club Associates, London

To my parents,
Cedric and Muriel Worsdell

Series designed by Paul Watkins

Layout by Sasha Rowntree

Filmset by Keyspools Limited, Golborne, Lancs
Printed and bound in Great Britain by
Morrison & Gibb Ltd, London & Edinburgh

Contents

Introduction

THE STORY OF EDWARD II has all the elements of drama. Not only through the eyes of Christopher Marlowe in his famous tragedy, but in real life also, the history of this unfortunate sovereign inclines one to wonder – and to pity. Surely Edward of Caernarvon, the first Prince of Wales, heir of the mighty King Edward I and his admirable consort Eleanor of Castile, was set from his earliest days to a career of substantial success and even glory. Regent for the kingdom in his father's absence at the age of fourteen, he succeeded to the throne in 1307 when he was twenty-three, not only a 'well proportioned and handsome person' but intelligent and courageous. Yet twenty years later his reign, punctuated by rebellion and civil war, was to terminate in an enforced abdication, followed by his death at the hands of the cruel assassins of Berkeley Castle, certainly the most ignominious fate endured by any British monarch.

It is Caroline Bingham's notable achievement that in a biography of striking narrative power, she breathes life into the character of Edward and does much to explain the measure of his failures. Inevitably much interest must concentrate on his sexual relationships, foremost amongst them the disastrous love affair with Piers Gaveston. Yet it was a connection which need not necessarily have offended against the conventional pattern of the age. The fifteen-year-old Gaveston, dashing, self-confident and amusing, a squire in the Royal Household, was a natural target for the friendship of the fourteen-year-old Edward; the chroniclers of the time frequently compared them to David and Jonathan, and Edward himself, a man who loved country sports, could row in the icy fens in the winter and even bathe there in February, could scarcely be termed effeminate in the modern sense of the word. It was then the indiscretion, the appalling obsessional recklessness with which Edward first as Prince then as King, pursued his passion, which was at fault and played its part in arousing the jealous opposition of the magnates of the kingdom. The same immoderate quality could be seen later in his patronage of the Despensers, father and son, and it is possible that in the rage of his slighted wife Queen Isabella, 'the She-Wolf of France', may be discerned a reflection of the same type of relationship with the young Hugh Despenser.

Nevertheless this is only part of Edward's story: the fascination of his life should not distract us from the equal interest of his times. He had after all inherited a double disadvantage from his famous father – a mountain of debts and a war with Scotland already turning against England on the one hand, and the legend of his predecessor's greatness on the other. Here Caroline Bingham, from the advantage of her specialised knowledge of Scottish history, is able to put the events leading up to the colossal English defeat at Bannockburn in 1314 properly in perspective from both sides. Domestically, the claims of his own nobles were of dubious constitutional validity, while their own aims remained strictly in favour of bolstering up their own powers. The Despensers themselves were responsible for much stable work of administration; as for the final rebellion, stage-managed by the Queen, by this time Isabella herself was scarcely the neglected bride of a generation back, but the fervent supporter of her own lover Mortimer. Was Edward after all the victim of fate rather than of his own nature? For even his own people, shortly after his death, showed their revulsion against its justice – and its manner – by a totally contrary movement for popular canonisation. After reading Caroline Bingham's skilful marshaling of the facts of scholarship and controversy on the subject, one can at least understand that point of view.

Antonia Fraser

Acknowledgments

Photographs and illustrations were supplied by or are reproduced by kind permission of the following: Aerofilms: 193; Batsford: 16, 73; Bibliotheque Nationale: *162*, *163*; Bodleian Library, Oxford: 94–5, 142; BPC: 79; Dean and Chapter of Bristol Cathedral: 56, 57; British Museum: *2*, *14*, *15*, 20/2, 21/2, 26, 27, 28, 31, 32, 33, 39, 44, 50, 52–3, 55/2, *68*, 71, 74, 75/2, *77/1*, *77/2*, 87, 90/1, 90/2, 91, 92, 98/1, 98/2, 105, 110–11, 112–13, 116/1, 116/2, 117/1, 117/2, 119, 122, 126, 129, 132, 136, 139, 144, 146–7, 152/1, 161, 167, 169, *174–5*, 189, *194/1*, *195*, 196, 199, *207*, 210, 210–11, 211, 213, 216; William Burrell Collection, Glasgow: 107; Dean and Chapter of Canterbury Cathedral, 184–5; Master and Fellows of Christ Church, Oxford: *206*; Courtauld Institute of Art: 23, 38; Crown Copyright (Department of the Environment): 179, (Edinburgh) 41, 103; Dean and Chapter of Durham Cathedral: 82; Michael Holford: *65*, *80/2*; A. F. Kersting: 48, 67, 84, 191, 201, 202/1, 202/2, 203; London Museum: 54, 194/2; National Monuments Record (Crown Copyright): 12, 20/1, 36, 75/1, 99, 109, 204, 214; National Portrait Gallery: 180; Phillips City Studio, Wells: 152/2; Pierpoint Morgan Library: 63; Pitkin Pictorials: 37; Public Record Office: 53, 183; Walter Scott, Bradford: 60, 155; Scottish Record Office: 86, 96; Edwin Smith: 21/1; Victoria and Albert Museum: *3*, 55/1, 55/3, *80/1*, 149, 153, 172, *173/1*, *173/2*, *173/3*; Reverend R. M. Ware: 19: Dean and Chapter of Westminster: 124, 176; Dean and Chapter of Winchester: 35; Rev. C. Woodforde: 166; Dean and Chapter of York: 10.

Numbers in italics refer to colour illustrations.

Picture research by Jane Dorner.

Maps and diagrams drawn by Design Practitioners Limited.

The details of the Bannockburn campaign have been the subject of controversy. The account in this book incorporates the conclusions of Professor G. W. S. Barrow, which the author has found the most convincing.

9

Edwardꞌ Primus · · · · · · · Edwardꞌ Sedꞌ

1 Edward, the King's Son 1284-1307

He was of a well-proportioned handsome person,
Of a courteous disposition, and well-bred,
And desirous of finding an occasion
To make proof of his strength.
He managed his steed wonderfully well.

(*Roll of Arms of the Princes, Barons and Knights*
who attended Edward I at the Siege of Caerlaverock.
Trans., Thomas Wright, 1864)

Edward I of England was a great King of his own people, and a scourge of his neighbours. He was the conqueror of Wales, though not perhaps of the Welsh, whose national identity has survived until the present time; he was the Hammer of the Scots – 'Scotorum Malleus' – in the words of the sixteenth-century epitaph on his tomb.

In the summer of 1307, Edward I, sixty-seven years of age and in failing health, set out upon his last campaign against the Scots. The invading army moved slowly north; slowly and yet more slowly as the King's strength failed him. On 3 July he left Carlisle, and on each of the next two days he progressed no more than two miles. By 6 July he had reached Burgh-upon-Sands, where he encamped, in preparation for the fording of the River Solway the following day. But on the morning of 7 July, when his servants came to help him from his bed, he fell dead, even as he attempted to rise.

The manner of his death sums up the man: in whatever he undertook he was indefatigable and indomitable. He was a King who stamped his personality upon his times; a King of whom men felt instinctively that in witnessing his death they were witnessing the end of an epoch. But a dead King, however dominant a personality he has been, does not remain the cynosure of a nation. As soon as Edward I was dead the attention of all men turned upon his eldest surviving son, Edward of Caernarvon, who, at the age of twenty-three became King Edward II.

The new King was not altogether an unknown figure. He had been heir to the throne since he was a few months old, and his upbringing had been designed to prepare him as perfectly as possible to be an able and conscientious successor to his father. On the whole, his adolescence and early manhood had been years of promise, and he seems to have succeeded his father with the goodwill of all the most influential of his subjects. The ecclesiastic who wrote the best contemporary account of him, the *Vita Edwardi Secundi*, and who referred to him as a Rehoboam succeeding a Solomon, was writing towards the end of the reign, in full possession of the advantage of hindsight.

Edward of Caernarvon, the fourth son of Edward I and his beloved Queen Eleanor of Castile, was born in the half-built

PREVIOUS PAGE Edward I and his son, Edward II, on the choir screen at York Minster.

OPPOSITE Statues of Edward I and his Queen, Eleanor of Castile, from Lincoln Cathedral.

LEFT Edward I makes his son Prince of Wales.

RIGHT Edward I rides into London on his return from a crusade.

62

A londres aunt ꝑ soiourner
Il ioec fu tot le ꝑner

Il ioec par maledie languist
Et morut ainꝺ dieu unsist
Il ioec esteit enseuelee
A westmouster ꝑ solempnite
Edward sun fiz apres regnast
Oil tuit la terre si le gardast
Oil fu de grant ꝓuestie
Oil meintint bien ses franchise
Ve seint Eglise a mult lamore
Rentes z possessions lour donet
A ꝺ poures freres de religion
Donent doua mult riche doun
Ven soit sun Realme menteneir

Caernarvon Castle was
still in the early stages
of building when Edward
was born there in 1284.

castle of Caernarvon on St Mark's day, 25 April 1284. St Mark's
day, a day of penitential processions, was regarded as an in-
auspicious day on which to be born. Nonetheless, two of the
three elder sons of Edward I and his Queen having died in
infancy, the birth of another Prince to secure the succession
could not be other than a matter for rejoicing.

In 1284, the heir to the throne of England was the eleven-
year-old Prince Alfonso, but, less than four months after the
birth of his younger brother, he died. Upon the infant, who
thus became heir to a warrior-statesman aged forty-five,
devolved the responsibility of fulfilling the expectations of a
demanding and formidable father.

It is a well-known story that Edward I, having promised the
vanquished Welsh a native-born Prince, presented to them his
newly-born son, a Prince born in Wales who could speak no
word of English. Unfortunately this is yet another example of

the historical fable which fails to survive the searchlight of thorough examination. Its first appearance is in John Stow's *Annales of England*, written in the reign of Elizabeth I, and furthermore, Edward of Caernarvon was not created Prince of Wales until 1301, shortly before he was seventeen. Nevertheless, even if he was not dedicated to the Welsh at the beginning of his life, Edward of Caernarvon was born among them, and perhaps if only for that reason the Welsh nourished an affection for him, and maintained their loyalty to him long after he had forfeited the affection and loyalty of his English subjects.

A Welshwoman named Mary Mawnsel was the young Prince's first wetnurse, but when she fell ill she was replaced by an English nurse, Alice Leygrave, whose usefulness enabled her to keep her employment long after the Prince had ceased to need a wetnurse. She became a permanent member of his household, and years later, after he became King, she was rewarded for many years of service both to him and to his Queen.

Edward of Caernarvon, more fortunate than his elder brothers, more fortunate indeed than the majority of medieval children, enjoyed excellent health. He grew up to be 'fair of body and great of strength', and even those chroniclers who could find few good words to say for his character never failed to write admiringly of his strength and his good looks. The various likenesses of him which survive testify to the truth of their words.

Edward's tutor was an elderly and highly respected knight named Sir Guy Ferre, whose position made him responsible for the general overseeing of Edward's education and welfare, not for giving the Prince his actual lessons. From Sir Guy Ferre, Edward may perhaps have learned the excellent horsemanship for which he was always admired, but which he preferred to employ in hunting and horse-racing, rather than in jousting, at which a medieval Prince was expected to excel.

As far as Edward's formal education was concerned, his attainments are not usually considered to have been high. Nonetheless, two languages would have been second nature to him, Norman-French, which was still the language of the Court, and English, which he required for conversing with the common people, whose company he enjoyed to an extent that nobles and ecclesiastics considered extraordinary. He would have learned some Latin. A medieval King was not expected to be a good Latin scholar, but Latin was the common language of European culture, and a King who wholly lacked it would have been disadvantageously under-educated for the purposes of diplomacy, correspondence, government business, and even for the basic necessities of religious observance. Edward is recorded as having borrowed – and not returned – books in Latin from the library of the monks of Canterbury. It has been said that this provides no proof that he was able to read Latin; all the same, a man's usual motive for borrowing a book is a desire to read it. Edward also purchased an illuminated *Life of St Thomas à Becket*. Perhaps he had a special devotion to St Thomas, for he was an assiduous pilgrim to his shrine at Canterbury. In the practice of religion Edward showed enthusiasm rather than merely dutiful observance, and he was always a generous patron of the Church, especially of the Dominican order.

As Edward grew up he developed a wide range of interests, some of which would have satisfied and others perturbed his stern father. Field sports and the breeding of horses and hounds, for which he had great enthusiasm, would have been considered very proper occupations for him. It may have been under his patronage that his chief huntsman, William Twick, wrote a treatise on hunting, *Le Art de Venerie*. An enjoyment of music would also have been considered proper enough. Professor Tout, one of Edward's severest critics, deprecatingly remarked that he was always attended on his travels by 'Genoese fiddlers'; but if this is expressed as 'Italian musicians' the implication is one of civilised taste rather than of frivolity. Besides enjoying the music of the Genoese, Edward also took great pleasure in the *crwth* or Celtic violin, so much so that he sent one of his household minstrels, Richard the Rhymer, to stay in the household of the Abbot of Shrewsbury where there was a good 'crouthere' who could teach him to play it.

All this was creditable enough. What struck contemporary and even later critics as deeply shocking was Edward's interest in rustic crafts. He mastered the skills of thatching, hedging and ditching and shoeing horses; but skills which provided the livelihoods of lesser men were considered highly improper matters for the attention of a prince or a king. And it was

Medieval Stringed Instruments

Edward was fond of music and was attended by 'Genoese fiddlers' on all his travels. Stringed instruments such as the gittern (right) were often portrayed in the art of the age.

BELOW Detail of the rybybe in Gloucester Cathedral.

ABOVE Wood carving in
Chichester Cathedral.
RIGHT Musicians from
Queen Mary's Psalter.

nothing short of scandalous that such an exalted personage should also enjoy rowing and swimming. No doubt he turned to these pursuits, as later kings and statesmen have done, as a relief from the stresses of public life, and he probably sought the company of ordinary people in the first place as a refuge from protocol and from the loneliness of his position.

Loneliness was indeed the basic experience of Edward's childhood. A sense of the remoteness of their parents was perhaps the common experience of most royal children; but Edward's parents were not merely remote, they were totally absent for a large part of his early childhood. In 1286, when his son was two years old, Edward I accompanied by his Queen went to France to do homage to the new King Philip IV for his French possessions, to settle disturbances in the English province of Gascony and to attend to many other matters which lie beyond the scope of this book. He remained abroad until 1289, when the five-year-old Edward of Caernarvon made his first public appearance, travelling from the royal manor of Langley in Hertfordshire to Dover, to welcome his parents after their three years' absence from England.

Three years is a long time to a very small child, and to Edward his parents must have seemed almost like strangers. But he had little time to re-establish a close relationship with his mother, for within fifteen months of her return to England she was dead. Eleanor of Castile had dedicated her life to her husband rather than her children. Indeed, a distinguished historian of the present century has described her as 'the best friend he ever had, a woman who won her way to the hearts of his subjects because she was ever ready to listen to the cry of the oppressed'. It was said that he never fully recovered from his sorrow at her death. His grief for her was made proverbial by his setting up the famous 'Eleanor crosses' at all the places where her funeral cortège rested on its way to her burial place at Westminster. Certainly in losing her he lost the one person who perhaps was capable of exerting a restraining influence upon the savage side of his nature, which became more apparent as he grew older; and probably Edward of Caernarvon lost the person who might have played most effectively the part of mediatrix between him and his father.

In the same year Edward lost his paternal grandmother,

22

Eleanor of Provence, who had always taken a kindly interest in his welfare, and since it was ten years before his father re-married, Edward's childhood was spent without anyone who might have occupied the place of his mother either in his affections or within the structure of the family.

During his boyhood it was a dwindling family as one by one his sisters were married off: Eleanor to the Duke of Bar, Margaret to the son of the Duke of Brabant, Joan to the Earl of Gloucester, Elizabeth to the Count of Holland, while Mary became a nun. Edward of course had no brothers until after his father's remarriage; but long before that event his own marriage had come under consideration.

It was first considered in 1290, when he was only six years old, and his prospective bride was Margaret, 'The Maid of Norway', grand-daughter and heiress of Alexander III, King of Scots, who had died in 1286.

The death of Alexander III was an event of great importance to both Scotland and England, because it provided Edward I with an opportunity to attempt to deal with Scotland as he had dealt with Wales, and thus it inaugurated the era of the Scottish War of Independence. It was also an event which overshadowed the life of Edward II, because it saddled him with a military and political problem which his father left unsolved and which he himself was to find wholly impossible of solution.

King Alexander's sons had predeceased him, and upon his death Scotland was faced with the prospect of a child Queen, the daughter of Alexander's daughter who had married the King of Norway. Edward I accordingly proposed a marriage between the little 'Maid of Norway' and Edward of Caernarvon, whereafter the two kingdoms of Scotland and England would be united under one monarchy. This was agreed by the Treaty of Birgham in 1290, which contained clauses stating that each country would continue to be responsible for its own internal affairs. But although the treaty safeguarded the legal system and governmental structure of Scotland, it is obvious enough that under the joint monarchy Scotland would have become the subordinate member of the partnership, as occurred centuries later after the Union of Crowns.

The death of the Maid of Norway frustrated the plans of Edward I and the proposed marriage of Edward of Caernarvon

The Royal House of Scotland

showing the claims of Balliol and Bruce

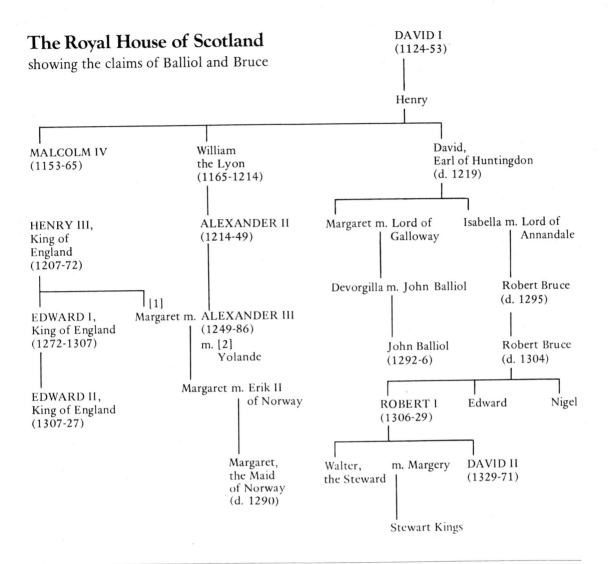

and left Scotland with the problem of a disputed succession. The claimants, however, played into the hands of the King of England, and unwary of the personal and national ambition which might colour his decision, desired him to act as arbitrator of their dispute.

Among many claimants the two whose claims left the rest out of count were John Balliol and Robert the Bruce (grandfather of the namesake who ultimately became King Robert I), both of whom were descendants of David I, King of Scots. The danger of the situation to Scotland's future lay in the fact that

The coronation of John
Balliol from a manuscript
dated *c.* 1310.

both Balliol and Bruce held lands in England for which they
owed homage to the English King. Both, in their ambition to
become King of Scots, would doubtless have been equally
willing to pay the price which Edward I demanded of the
successful competitor: that the man who became King of Scots
should do homage not only for his English estates but also for his
kingdom. Overlordship of Scotland was an ancient claim on the
part of English kings: Henry II had managed to enforce it when
he captured the Scottish King William the Lion, but Richard

Cœur-de-Lion had renounced it again in return for a cash payment in 1189. There the matter might justly have ended.

However, John Balliol, who emerged as the successful competitor from Edward 1's arbitration tribunal, and was crowned King of Scots at Scone on St Andrew's day, 30 November 1292, unhappily for himself and for his countrymen, submitted to Edward's demand and paid homage for his kingdom.

With 'legalism bordering on contempt', Edward 1 underlined

John Balliol does homage to Edward 1. By this act the King of Scots became the vassal of the King of England.

Balliol's vassal status, and the consequence was that three years later the unhappy King of Scots renounced his allegiance to Edward and allied himself with France.

Edward retaliated with an invasion of Scotland. First he made an object lesson of the prosperous port of Berwick, which he sacked with a savagery from which it never recovered. Next he defeated Balliol in a battle near Dunbar, after which the defeated King was forced to surrender both his crown and his kingdom in an ignominious ceremony at Brechin on 11 July 1296. He was carried prisoner to England, but ultimately allowed to depart from the political scene and from history to a quiet end in France.

Edward I took back with him to England the regalia of Scotland and the Stone of Destiny, on which the kings of Scots had hitherto been crowned; though a legend persisted that what he took with him was a supposititious stone. Edward I might have made and unmade a King and taken away the symbols of sovereignty, but a new crown would be made for a new King in the course of time. For the present Edward supposed that Scotland had gone the way of Wales, and he turned his attention to another neighbour with whom his relations had deteriorated of recent years.

The question of homage bedevilled the relations of England and France as much as it did those of England and Scotland. Philip IV of France, though he laid no claims to the kingdom of England, was greatly concerned to exert all his rights of suzerainty over the lands which Edward I held from him in France, and eager to reduce if possible, the territories of a too-powerful vassal.

Edward I's response to the pressure put upon him by the King of France was to threaten Philip with an alliance of inimical neighbours encircling his kingdom. In the interests of this anti-French policy the marriage of Edward of Caernarvon was arranged for a second time. He was betrothed to Philippa, daughter of the French King's enemy the Count of Flanders.

Edward I himself proposed to lead an invasion of France by way of Flanders, while the Earls of Hereford and Norfolk were to lead a second invasion through Gascony. During the absence of the King, Edward of Caernarvon, who was thirteen in 1297, was to make his political début as nominal Regent of England,

OPPOSITE John Balliol on board ship. After his enforced abdication in 1296 Balliol was imprisoned in England but subsequently permitted to retire to France.

though actual responsibility would be in the hands of a Regency Council. However, before Edward I was able to leave England he was obliged to deal with domestic problems which in some ways foreshadowed the problems his son was to encounter.

Constant warfare necessitated constant demands for money, and the financial exactions which preceded the King's invasion of France led to widespread discontent. The Archbishop of Canterbury, Robert Winchelsey, resisted the payment of civil taxes by the clergy without the express approval of the Pope, and Edward I's struggle with Winchelsey was at the point of deadlock while the French expedition was in preparation. The King was prevented from dealing with the primate as forcefully as he might otherwise have done by a simultaneous though unconnected quarrel with his nobility. Hitherto Edward I had been largely successful in carrying the magnates of England with him in all the enterprises he had undertaken. Nonetheless, an undercurrent of discontent had been steadily growing. The resentment of the magnates had been aroused partly by the taxation to which they had been subjected to finance the King's wars, partly it stemmed from the great legal reforms which Edward I had carried out during the earlier years of his reign. With the intention of increasing the scope of royal justice and of providing homogeneity of law throughout the land, the King had curtailed baronial jurisdictions and abolished many baronial privileges and franchises. Inevitably there was a legacy of bitterness. The magnates also nourished a grievance at the King's increased use of mercenary soldiers, which limited their own power in time of war by reducing the usefulness of the feudal levy. And the Marcher Lords as a separate group were resentful of the decline of their influence which had resulted from the conquest of Wales.

The Earls of Norfolk and Hereford, the proposed leaders of the Gascony expedition, emerged as the spearheads of the opposition when they refused to lead the invasion force, claiming that, as Earl Marshal and Constable of England respectively, it was their privilege to accompany the King to war. The use they made of office and privilege as a means of opposing the King's designs prefigures some of the political manœuvrings of Thomas of Lancaster, the leader of the opposition to Edward of Caernarvon in the next reign.

OPPOSITE Edward I with monks and bishops. The King's pressing need for money to support his wars led him into conflict with Robert Winchelsey, Archbishop of Canterbury, who resisted the payment of civil taxes by the clergy.

Norfolk and Hereford were strong enough to force the King to abandon the Gascony expedition, though he persisted in his determination to invade France through Flanders. Having reached a compromise with Winchelsey, Edward I was able to conceal his defeat at the hands of the magnates with a spectacular face-saving ceremony.

On 14 July 1297, Edward I appeared on a specially built dais outside Westminster Hall and made a public oration in which he apologised for the heavy taxation which he had exacted but explained that it had been imposed for the ultimate good of his people. He then appealed for public support in the forthcoming

ABOVE Edward I returning from Gascony, from an early fifteenth-century manuscript.
RIGHT Edward II as a child with two bishops. The scene may represent his recognition as his father's heir, or as Regent during his absence.

32

war, in which he must hazard and might lose his life for their sakes. He concluded by demanding that all the magnates present should come forward and swear fealty to Edward of Caernarvon as their future King. This they did. It is unfortunately impossible to know how much of the background to this solemn but somewhat hollow ceremony the Prince knew and understood.

The following month Edward I departed for France, leaving his son to preside over the Regency Council and to experience the flavour if not the full reality of authority and responsibility. He was to experience also a foretaste of the multifarious problems which beset a King who was expected to rule personally as well as to reign.

It was fortunate for Edward of Caernarvon that his regency did not carry full responsibility, for he was left with a situation which would have taxed the ability of the most experienced statesman. Edward I had left a country in which popular discontent was widespread and vociferous, the chief causes being the heavy taxation on wool by which the King had raised money for his invasion of France, and his demand for huge quantities of grain and meat which each county had been called upon to produce to provision the army. The discontent expressed itself in bitter verses threatening revolt if a leader should arise.

Happily for Edward I and his son the last years of the thirteenth century bred no Wat Tyler, and between the popular unrest and the baronial opposition there was little enough common cause. England was near to the brink of civil war, but the causes of trouble were too fragmented to bring it about. Instead of civil war the government was called upon to face a new resurgence of trouble in Scotland led by Sir William Wallace.

In September 1297, the month after Edward I's departure for Flanders, the Earl of Surrey, whom he had left in charge of Scottish affairs, was overwhelmingly defeated by Wallace at Stirling Bridge. The English occupying forces lost their hold upon all Scotland between the Forth and the Tweed, and Berwick was reoccupied by the Scots. The army sent north by the Regency Council managed to retake Berwick at the beginning of 1298, when Edward I announced his impending return to deal with the intransigence of the Scots once for all.

33

Defeat at the hands of the Scots was not the only defeat that Edward I was obliged to digest before the close of 1297. Before he had departed to Flanders the party of the two Earls had presented to the King a list of their 'Maunstrances' or grievances, with which the Regency Council had been empowered to deal in his absence. The result was the famous 'Confirmation of the Charters', the charters in question being Magna Carta and the Charter of the Forest, documents intended initially to set out and secure baronial privileges, though later history vastly increased their scope and significance. The Confirmation obliged Edward I to abjure the right to levy taxes of all kinds without the 'will and assent of the Church, the earls, barons, knights, burgesses and other free men of the kingdom', words which grew in significance with the elaboration of democratic theories.

Winchelsey and the earls, by pursuing their separate quarrels at a time when the King was embroiled in foreign war, rather than by concerted action, had won a resounding victory for which Edward I never forgave them. The Confirmation of the Charters, sealed by the King at Ghent on 5 November 1297, was an example of the defeat of a king by baronial opposition which may have had a profound effect upon the mind of Edward of Caernarvon. He was soon to observe that his father did not regard as binding an agreement made under duress; he was to witness his father extricate himself from the limitations imposed upon him by diplomatic chicanery, an example which he was not slow to follow.

Edward I returned from a campaign which had been militarily inconclusive to face troubles at home, a disappointed man aged by a multiplicity of conflicts. A truce with France robbed the Flemish alliance of its purpose, and the betrothal of Edward of Caernarvon and the daughter of the Count of Flanders was broken off. The detaching of France from alliance with Scotland gave point to continuing peaceful relations with Philip IV, and in 1299, by the Treaty of Montreuil, Edward I contracted to marry the seventeen-year-old sister of the French King, while Edward of Caernarvon was betrothed to his daughter. At the end of the year, the King of England, white-haired and older in appearance than his sixty years, married Margaret of France in Canterbury Cathedral. The Prince would have to wait

34

some years for his French bride, who was only eight years old.

The distant prospect of marriage, however, was of much less interest to him than a new relationship formed after the return of his father from Flanders.

On his campaign of 1297, Edward I had been accompanied by a Gascon knight Sir Arnaud de Gaveston, an old companion-in-arms who had been captured by the French earlier in the reign, and had escaped the year before the Flanders expedition in time to join the English King, bringing with him his son Piers, who was about fifteen years old. While he was in Flanders, Edward I had appointed Piers Gaveston a squire of the Royal Household, and evidently he had made an excellent impression, for in 1298 the King appointed him one of the ten *pueri in custodia*, royal wards who were the official companions of the King's son. A chronicler writing about thirty years later described the beginning of the fateful relationship between Piers Gaveston and Edward of Caernarvon. Piers was presented, 'and when the King's son saw him he fell so much in love that he entered upon an enduring compact with him, and chose and determined to knit an indissoluble bond of affection with him, before all other mortals'.

No contemporary or near-contemporary likeness of Piers Gaveston exists. As far as written estimates of his character are

An effigy in Winchester Cathedral traditionally identified as that of Piers Gaveston's father, Sir Arnaud de Gaveston, a respected companion-in-arms to Edward I.

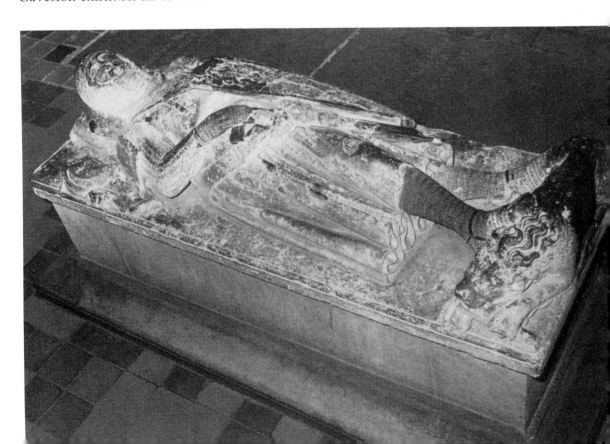

RIGHT Edward II's
stepmother, Margaret of
France, was only two years
his senior. She might have
made him a wiser and more
tolerant consort than her
niece Isabella, 'the she-wolf
of France'.

OPPOSITE A queen's head
from Beverley Minster
which may represent
Isabella of France, who
married Edward in 1308.

concerned, though they are mostly condemnatory they reveal
that he was handsome and amusing, possessed of boundless
self-confidence and devoid of innate reverence for rank, and
that he excelled at martial sports. An impression emerges of a
young man of vivid personality and considerable charm, one
who might with equal facility make himself loved or hated. It
was his fate to be loved beyond discretion by Edward of
Caernarvon, and hated with commensurable ferocity by almost
every other influential man in England. Edward I would no

doubt have disapproved of the emotional intensity of the relationship between his son and Gaveston if he had been aware of it; but for the time being it went unnoticed, for the King had many problems awaiting his attention.

In the early summer of 1298, the King marched north, and on 22 July he utterly defeated the Scots, led by Wallace, at the battle of Falkirk. Wallace, who escaped from the field, betook himself to France in search of French help, but his hopes were disappointed by the diplomacy of the English King. Two royal marriages between France and England were to keep the Franco-Scottish alliance in abeyance for many years.

While the King was occupied with warfare in the north, Edward of Caernarvon, released from the responsibility or at least partial responsibility of regency, was free for the last time in his life to enjoy himself without restraint or criticism. He divided his time between London, Windsor and the manor of Langley.

At Langley, later called King's Langley in honour of his liking for the place, Edward had spent some of the happiest times of his childhood, and it became his favourite residence. It was a pleasant manor, not far from St Albans, built on the banks of the River Gade, where there were two little islands and two water-mills. It had eight acres of parkland in which roe deer were kept, and one hundred and twenty acres of farmland. But it was something more than a farm: vines grew in the gardens, and the stables housed a camel. The manor-house itself possessed both elegance and comfort; the great hall was decorated with a mural depicting knights on their way to a tournament, and there were fireplaces in the bedchambers. At Langley Edward could enjoy indoor comforts or indulge in the rustic pleasures to which he was so unsuitably addicted; but it is worth remarking that his enjoyment of the outdoors, even of 'sport in the water' was not confined to summer weather. It is on record that he went rowing in the Fens at Christmas time

A game with sticks and a ball such as Edward and Gaveston might have played at King's Langley.

39

and swimming during the usually unkind month of February.

Edward's freedom ended soon after his father's marriage to Margaret of France in 1299. The following year his father decided that he should have his first experience of warfare in a new Scottish campaign.

The campaign of 1300 took Edward I and his son to the south-western corner of Scotland, where William Wallace had found strong support. Before the march north began in earnest, both the King and the Prince stayed at the Abbey of Bury St Edmunds. When the King left, before he had gone far on his way, he sent back his standard, with the request that Mass should be said upon it, and that it should be touched with every holy relic that the Abbey possessed. The Abbey's chronicler was much impressed by this pious act, but even more impressed by the devoutness of Edward of Caernarvon who stayed at the Abbey a week longer than his father. 'He became our brother in chapter,' wrote the monk. 'Every day, moreover, he asked to be served with a monk's portion such as the brothers take in refectory.'

On 18 May he left Bury St Edmunds, and by 25 June he had reached Carlisle. From Carlisle the King and his son advanced to besiege Caerlaverock Castle. The herald-poet who compiled the *Roll of Arms of the Princes, Barons and Knights who attended Edward I at the Siege of Caerlaverock* recorded that 'Edward the King's Son' had command of the rearguard of the English army, and wrote admiringly of his looks, his horsemanship and his desire to distinguish himself.

Caerlaverock Castle fell after a siege of five days, but apart from a single skirmish in which the Prince was considered to have acquitted himself well, the campaign offered no opportunities for winning renown, for the Scots prudently declined to offer battle. The King of England's irritation with the whole campaign was increased when Archbishop Winchelsey arrived with a message from the Pope censuring the King's imperialism towards Scotland. 'By the Blood of God,' the King replied, in a violent outburst of anger, '... and for Jerusalem's sake I will not rest, nay, rather I will defend my right so long as the breath of life sustains my body.' Nonetheless, when the autumn came, the English army retired south again. Christmas was spent at Northampton, and in January Edward of Caernarvon returned

to Langley. Throughout the campaign Gaveston had been with him. They remained as inseparable as David and Jonathan, to whom the chroniclers frequently compared them.

It appeared, however, that the King had been well pleased with his son's conduct in Scotland, even if the campaign itself had been disappointing. Paternal approval was handsomely displayed on 7 February 1301 when, at a Parliament in Lincoln, Edward of Caernarvon received the titles and endowments of Prince of Wales and Earl of Chester. The extent of the Principality of Wales can be seen on the map on page 134. The rest of Wales was held by the Marcher Lords, who, though their power had been greatly reduced by the conquests of Edward I, remained an influential independent group, even if their lands no longer constituted a buffer state between wild Wales and the kingdom of England.

1301 saw renewed campaigning in Scotland, and, as an

Caerlaverock Castle, which fell to Edward and his father after a siege of five days.

additional mark of his father's approval and confidence, Edward of Caernarvon was given command of half the English army. The King was to invade on the east by way of Berwick, the Prince on the west by way of Carlisle. Though the Prince had an independent command he was expected to rely upon the advice of an experienced soldier, Henry de Lacy, Earl of Lincoln. He was accompanied also by the Earl of Hereford, now reconciled with the King, by Ralph de Monthermer, the second husband of his sister Joan, Countess of Gloucester, and by his cousin Thomas of Lancaster. Piers Gaveston was also with him.

The campaign of 1301 turned out to be as unpropitious as that of the previous year. The Scots followed their prudent policy of avoiding pitched battle, and the English, from their own viewpoint, 'achieved nothing glorious or praiseworthy'. The onset of winter brought savage weather, and at the end of the campaigning season both the Prince and Gaveston required the services of a physician.

During the year 1302 the King of England left the Scots in peace, but his policy was merely to gather his resources in readiness for a new effort. Preparations were again in hand at the beginning of 1303, and they were stimulated by the news of a defeat suffered by the King's Lieutenant in Scotland, Sir Thomas Segrave, who was surprised and taken prisoner at Roslin in February.

In readiness for the invasion Edward of Caernarvon amassed great quantities of tents, weapons and armour for the men under his command, and ordered banners to be made bearing his own arms and the emblems of St Edward the Confessor, St Edmund and St George. The Prince set out from London on 13 March, and both he and his father were in Scotland by the middle of May.

This year the King's intention was to march the length of Scotland in force, spreading destruction and terror, to avenge the defeat inflicted upon Segrave, and to illustrate to the whole country the uselessness of further resistance. The King's northward march took him as far as Kinloss on the Moray Firth, and then south again by way of Dundee, Scone and Dunblane. The Prince wintered at Perth and the King at Dunfermline. A similar march to illustrate superior strength and to spread destruction had been made by the Roman Emperor Severus eleven centuries before; Edward I did as much and achieved as little lasting effect. At the time, however, he may have supposed that he had finally crushed his enemies. In the spring of 1304, many prominent Scottish lords surrendered to him, and by the summer he was sufficiently satisfied with the results of his year's campaigning to return again to England. He even ordered his Exchequer, which had been stationed at York for over six years, to return to its customary headquarters at Westminster.

In the autumn he decided that the Prince of Wales should go to France and do homage for Aquitaine on his behalf. Towards the end of October the Prince went to Dover in readiness to make the crossing, but the French King failed to send either the escort or the safe conduct which he had promised. Accordingly, with the approval of the King, the Prince declined to go. It was a question of prestige at stake, and not of reluctance on his part. Relieved of the need to deputise for his father he retired to enjoy himself at Langley.

Since he had made his political début in his nominal regency when he was thirteen the Prince had served an increasingly exacting apprenticeship and to all appearances he had measured up to his responsibilities in a way that had fully satisfied his father. Yet it is impossible to avoid the suspicion that there must have been something wrong with this apparently excellent relationship, that there must have been tensions and problems too unspecific to find their way into the chronicles of the period. 1304 had ended with apparently perfect harmony between father and son; 1305 was a year of violent discord, seemingly caused by a relatively insignificant matter.

On 14 June Edward of Caernarvon was banished from Court, and the Exchequer forbidden to provide him with the means of financial support. The cause of the King's violent anger against his son was reported to have been a quarrel between the Prince and Walter Langton, Bishop of Coventry and Lichfield, at that time the King's favourite minister; and according to one account the quarrel had arisen from the Bishop's natural anger that the Prince, with Gaveston and others, had broken into his park and poached his deer. However, banishment and the accompanying financial penalties seems an extraordinarily heavy punishment for a relatively trivial offence, for which a reprimand followed by apology and restitution would surely

43

A lady hunting a stag from Queen Mary's Psalter. The Psalter is named after Mary Tudor who owned it in the sixteenth century, but it dates from *c.* 1308.

have been sufficient punishment, unaccompanied by public humiliation. Possibly the King may have felt that merely because the culprit was his son he should not seem to err in leniency towards him; or he may have felt that in the heir to the throne any action tinged with irresponsibility must be shown to be utterly impermissible. Nonetheless, the King appears unnecessarily heavy-handed in his treatment of the offence, and it seems a likely explanation that his anger with the Prince came as the culmination of some build-up of tension between them.

The Prince was deprived of Gaveston's company, and it was the end of July before he felt able to write to his stepmother asking her to persuade the King to allow him to see Gaveston and Gilbert de Clare, the son of his sister Joan. Margaret of France must have been a remarkably tactful young woman, for she and her stepson, who was only two years her junior, managed to maintain a pleasantly affectionate relationship without arousing the jealousy of the old King. Whether she interceded with him successfully on this occasion is not known.

The Prince's banishment from Court enabled him to discover who were his true friends. The Treasurer of his Household, Walter Reynolds, helped him financially, so did his old tutor Sir Guy Ferre, and so did Anthony Bec, Bishop of Durham, who was on bad terms with the King. Another supporter at this time, and a loyal servant in the future, was Sir Hugh Despenser the elder. Edward of Caernarvon did not forget those who had helped him when he needed it; if some of them had gambled on his future gratitude they proved to have made the right choice.

While the Prince was out of favour the King had other matters than his son's doings to preoccupy him. He was busy making arrangements for the future government of Scotland, and when William Wallace was betrayed and captured in August he might justifiably have felt that he had received the final assurance that there would be no further trouble in the north. If Wallace had been left to rot in prison the end of a heroic career would most likely have been oblivion. But the King, determined to punish commensurably though unjustly the trouble he had caused, inflicted upon him the public butchery of a traitor's death, and thus inadvertently provided the cause of Scottish independence with a martyr. In no time an apparently dead cause was shown to be very much alive.

Robert the Bruce, grandson of Balliol's rival and inheritor of his claim, had long vacillated between allegiance to the King of England and adherence to a claim which Balliol's kingship seemed to have set aside. In 1304 he had been reconciled with Edward I, but by the end of 1305 he was contemplating adopting the cause for which Wallace had fought and died. Balliol was a disgraced exile, Scotland though seemingly in subjection was seething with discontent, and Bruce's claim could be made good if enough men would be willing to fight for him. It was revived in the most dramatic fashion at the beginning of 1306, when Bruce met his enemy and Balliol's kinsman, John Comyn, Lord of Badenoch, in the Greyfriars Church at Dumfries. Possibly his plan had been to attempt to win Comyn to his cause, but a quarrel ensued, and Comyn was stabbed to death before the high altar. Since Comyn also had been reconciled to the English King in 1304 the sacrilegious murder proclaimed Robert the Bruce as the King's enemy. For him the revival of the war with England had three possibilities: he would die in battle, or die as Wallace had done, or he would emerge as King of Scots. He declared himself at once, and making a great bid for popular support, he had himself crowned at Scone in March 1306. He possessed neither the crown nor the Stone of

Destiny, but a golden 'coronella' and a throne were substituted for the missing symbols of sovereignty. Upon receiving the news of the coronation, the King of England at once prepared for war.

It did not augur well for Robert the Bruce, for Edward I was in a stronger position for making war than he had been for some years. At the end of 1305 the new Pope Clement V had absolved him from his oath to abide by the Confirmation of the Charters. It was a slippery way to escape from the limitations imposed upon him by the baronage, and it provided Edward of Caernarvon with a useful if undesirable precedent. Clement V, elevated to the papacy from the archbishopric of Bordeaux, was a Gascon, and therefore born a subject of the English King. Edward I found his inborn pro-Englishness useful in other ways than providing absolution from his oath; he at once induced the Pope to rid him of his troublesome primate, Archbishop Winchelsey, by summoning him to Rome. Winchelsey remained out of the country until after the accession of Edward of Caernarvon. Edward I had rid himself of the very opposition which had hampered him in 1297, besides which France was now his ally. It seemed that Robert the Bruce could scarcely have asserted his claim at a more unpropitious moment.

In the meantime a reconciliation had taken place between Edward I and his son. In October 1305, after four months' absence from Court, the Prince was received by his father, and his return to favour signalised by his presiding at a great banquet in Westminster Hall.

As though to illustrate that the trouble of 1305 implied no stigma of continuing disapproval, the King knighted his son in the spring of 1306 before the renewal of the Scottish war. The Prince was further honoured by a grant of the duchy of Aquitaine and other territories, and he himself knighted 297 noble youths in Westminster Abbey. At the banquet that followed, upon a pair of swans imprisoned in a net of gold, the old King took an oath that when he had defeated Robert the Bruce he would go on a Crusade, and the Prince swore that he would never sleep twice in one place until he had reached Scotland and avenged the death of Comyn. Other oath-takers followed them, all pledging themselves to variations upon the theme of the defeat of Bruce.

46

The campaign was successful, though by no means con-
clusive. Edward I himself played little part in it, for his health
had begun to fail him. Before he himself reached Scotland
Bruce had been defeated by Aymer de Valence, Earl of
Pembroke, at the battle of Methven. Bruce escaped, and
Pembroke and the Prince of Wales laid siege to Kildrummy
Castle in which Bruce's Queen, his sister, his daughter, and
Isabel of Fife, Countess of Buchan, who had crowned him in
accordance with the privilege of her family, had taken refuge.

The castle fell, and at the orders of Edward I the Countess of
Buchan and Bruce's sister were imprisoned in wooden cages
exposed on the walls of the castles of Berwick and Roxburgh.
Though no act of equal savagery was ever imputed to Edward
of Caernarvon, it was said that in this campaign he showed himself merciless to the enemy. 'Stark', or grim, is the adjective
applied to him by John Barbour, author of the great epic poem
The Bruce:

> The eldest and apparent heir,
> A young bachelor, stark and fair,
> Sir Edward called of Carnarvirnane,
> That was the starkest man of ane
> That men find might in any country;
> The Prince of Wales that time was he.

The year ended with Bruce a hunted fugitive, but still free, and
King in name. In January 1307, when Parliament assembled at
Carlisle, the papal nuncio solemnly excommunicated him.

In the meantime the King and his son wintered at Lanercost
Priory near Carlisle, and at Lanercost a new outbreak of trouble
occurred between them. The most circumstantial account of the
incident relates that the Prince requested his father to bestow on
Piers Gaveston the title of Count of Ponthieu, which was a title
of his own. It might from his own viewpoint have seemed a
reasonable request; the territorial endowment was not large,
the title but one of many now that he was Prince of Wales,
Duke of Aquitaine and Earl of Chester. The old King saw it in a
very different light. His answer was 'You baseborn whoreson!
Do you want to give lands away now, you who never gained
any? As the Lord lives, if it were not for fear of breaking up the
kingdom you should never enjoy your inheritance!' He

Lanercost Priory in Cumberland where Edward and
his father spent the winter of 1307 and quarrelled over
the title Edward wished to bestow on Gaveston.

emphasised his words by tearing out a handful of his son's hair and driving him from his presence.

Evidently the Prince's love for Gaveston had now come to his notice and seriously alarmed him, and the consequence of the Prince's rash request was Gaveston's banishment. He was ordered to leave England by the end of April, and he and the Prince were both made to swear upon the Host that the King's command would be obeyed. Having sworn, the Prince was permitted to escort him to Dover. Nonetheless, Gaveston's banishment carried no accompanying penalties. He was granted a generous allowance and ordered merely to stay away until recalled, presumably until the King judged that his son's feelings had cooled, or possibly until marriage had altered the direction of his affections. The King, having formed a good opinion of Gaveston in the first place, did not relinquish it; his son was the person whose folly he blamed. But, though he might part the Prince and Gaveston for the time being, little time was left him in which to exercise authority. In the spring of 1307 he was a dying man.

The Prince was doubtless well aware of this, and he came as near to showing contempt for his father's orders as he dared, for he detained Gaveston until the beginning of May, and told him not to go to Gascony as the King had commanded him, but to Ponthieu.

When he had gone, loaded with presents, the Prince regretfully turned north to join his father in a new campaign in Scotland. While the dying King made his way slowly north and the reluctant Prince followed him, Robert the Bruce won his first victory, defeating Aymer de Valence at the battle of Loudon Hill.

By the beginning of July the Prince had not caught up with his father, and the King had not quite reached the Border. Indomitable to the last, Edward I struggled as far as the ford of the Solway at Burgh-upon-Sands. With his death, on the morning of 7 July, Edward of Caernarvon became King of England, and inherited besides the kingdom a mountain of debts and a war in which the tide had turned against him.

2 The King and Piers Gaveston 1307-13

*I do not remember to have heard
that one man so loved another.*

(*Vita Edwardi Secundi*)

KING EDWARD I, in the words of a twentieth-century historian, 'had played his role magnificently, offending none of the conventions of his age'. Though the magnates of England might have resented and opposed certain aspects of his policy, as a man and as a King they had respected him.

As heir to his father's greatness King Edward II had a great deal to live up to. At the same time he had a very difficult inheritance, for the expense of war with Scotland had enormously overstrained the resources of the Crown. The old King left over £60,000 of debts. He had borrowed heavily from the Florentine banking-houses of Bardi and Frescobaldi; soldiers, officials and tradesmen were unpaid, and the Exchequer accounts were hopelessly in arrears. Edward II inherited the unhappy obligation of imposing order upon this chaos, while at the same time he was expected to continue the war. His situation was somewhat like that of James VI and I when he succeeded Elizabeth I: he was expected to be a worthy heir to his predecessor's greatness, while hampered by being also the inheritor of that predecessor's unsolved problems. It was said that Edward II's accession was greeted with 'exceptional rejoicing'. He himself was perhaps the person who had least reason to rejoice.

The problems which faced him, however, were not uppermost in Edward's mind when he received the news of his father's death. His first act was to recall the exiled Gaveston.

The new King sent his father's corpse to Waltham Abbey to await interment, while he himself went to Carlisle to receive the homage of all the English magnates who had been with his father in the north. Thence he went to Dumfries to receive the homage of such Scottish lords as still adhered to their English allegiance. Gaveston joined him at Dumfries, and there, on 6 August, Edward created him Earl of Cornwall, a title customarily given to a member of the royal family and supported by a great territorial endowment which included many estates beyond the boundaries of the county of Cornwall. It would have been more appropriate if Edward had granted the earldom of Cornwall to one of his young half-brothers, Thomas of Brotherton and Edmund of Woodstock, the sons of his father by Margaret of France. It was not surprising, therefore, that the elevation of Gaveston with which Edward dramatically

52

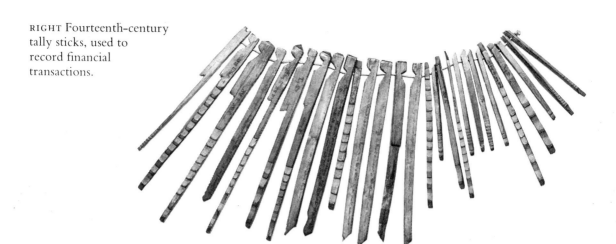

RIGHT Fourteenth-century tally sticks, used to record financial transactions.

Facsimiles of medieval tiles showing companions playing music and picking fruit.

began his reign, was, in the words of his most recent biographer, 'a prodigious shock to the contemporary establishment'.

The chroniclers who wrote of Edward and Gaveston appear to have had no doubt that their relationship was one of love, not friendship. 'Anon he had home his love Piers of Gaveston,' wrote one of them, '... and did him great reverence, and worshipped and made him great and rich. Of this doing fell villainy to the lover, evil speech and backbiting to the love, slander to the people, harm and damage to the realm.'

The author of the *Vita Edwardi Secundi*, expressing himself in a more balanced and judicious manner, wrote: 'I do not remember to have heard that one man so loved another. Jonathan cherished David, Achilles loved Patroclus. But we do not read that they were immoderate. Our King, however, was incapable of moderate favour, and on account of Piers was said to forget himself, and so Piers was accounted a sorcerer.'

Edward II lived in a period when an intimate friendship between two men was a formal relationship governed by a code of rules like that of Courtly Love. Such a relationship was the subject of an Anglo-Norman romance, *Amis and Amiloun*. Two friends could be described as *'leals amants'* (loyal lovers) and their relationship as *'fyne amour'*, but homosexuality was completely outside the convention. Although the chronicler of the Abbey of Meaux condemned Edward II for being 'too much given to sodomy', of the precise nature of his relations with Gaveston there is no evidence at all. But by the 'immoderateness' of his behaviour, Edward gave encouragement to such accusations, and thereby he did what his father had never done – he offended

54

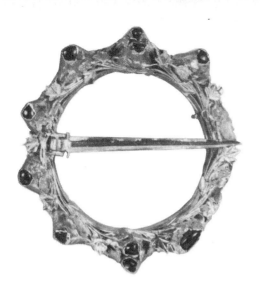

the conventions of his age, and offended them outrageously.

'Evil speech and backbiting' might nonetheless have been the only consequence if the King's love for Gaveston had not had adverse effects upon the political situation. The King's greatest folly was his failure to draw the line between a private affair and public affairs.

In the early autumn of 1307, by the time he had despatched his father's corpse south and received the homage of his lords, the campaigning season was virtually at an end. Accordingly, Edward appointed his cousin John of Brittany, Earl of Richmond, and Aymer de Valence, Earl of Pembroke, to take charge of Scottish affairs, while he himself went south to meet his first Parliament and to attend the burial of his father.

Parliament, held at Northampton in October, agreed to the provision of funds for the old King's burial and the new King's marriage and coronation, which were to follow fast upon it. The burial took place on 27 October in Westminster Abbey, the King's marriage was arranged for the new year. In the meantime Edward married Gaveston to his niece Margaret de Clare, daughter of his sister Joan, Countess of Gloucester. This exalted marriage was scarcely less of a shock to the nobility of England than Gaveston's elevation to the earldom of Cornwall. But one shock followed another. In January 1308, when Edward II went to France to be married, Gaveston was appointed Regent. If Edward had deliberately set out to insult and alienate his lords he could scarcely have done so more effectively.

The marriage of Edward II and Isabella of France took place at Boulogne on 25 January, and to both French and English the

Medieval jewels such as Edward might have given to Gaveston. He was prodigal in his generosity to his favourite and his gifts included some of the best jewels from the dowry of his wife, Isabella of France.
ABOVE LEFT Gold brooch set with rubies of a late thirteenth-century design.
ABOVE RIGHT A gold brooch of the fourteenth century.
ABOVE An English late thirteenth-century gold ring.

marriage seemed a splendid and joyous event. The French were as much impressed by the handsome young King as the English were by his bride, who was described as *'des beales la rose'* – the fairest of the fair.

The coronation, which followed on 25 February in Westminster Abbey, was disastrous. Gaveston, to whom had been accorded the privilege of carrying the crown, appeared dressed in royal purple sewn with pearls, 'so decked out that he more resembled the god Mars than an ordinary mortal'; and at the coronation banquet the King was so indiscreet in displaying his preference for Gaveston's company that the Queen's uncles, who had escorted her to England, departed in dudgeon to report to the King of France that Edward was more in love with his favourite than with his wife. They had good reason to say so, for Edward had presented to Gaveston the best of Isabella's jewels and the wedding presents.

Roof bosses in Bristol Cathedral representing Edward II (above) and Isabella of France.

56

That 'exceptional rejoicing' which had accompanied the accession of Edward II, and the goodwill of the nobility which he had enjoyed at the outset of his reign, had by now evaporated, and for this the indiscretion of the King and the offensive conduct of Gaveston were principally to blame.

Gaveston had obviously conducted himself with the greatest circumspection in front of the old King, to whom he owed the promising beginning of his career, and for whose awesome presence and uncertain temper he must have had as much respect and fear as everyone else. But once he emerged as the new King's favourite, as the Earl of Cornwall, and as the Regent in the King's absence, all circumspection was cast away, and Gaveston's naturally high opinion of himself became the most overweening arrogance. Then, wrote the King's contemporary biographer, 'the magnates of the land hated him because he alone found favour in the King's eyes and lorded it over them like a second King, to whom all were subject and none equal'. Edward, who could not do enough to exalt his 'idol', did nothing to restrain him, and indeed, the more unpopular Gaveston became 'the greater grew his love and tenderness' towards him.

However, Gaveston's enemies shortly found that they possessed an effective means of taking action against him. At his coronation Edward had taken a newly-formulated version of the coronation oath. It contained a fourth clause in addition to the usual three, in which the King swore to be held by the just laws and customs that the community of the realm should determine. Probably these words had been formulated not with future developments in mind, but with the recollection of Edward I's adroit extrication of himself from his oath to observe the Confirmation of the Charters. However, this fourth clause was found very much to the purpose by those lords who wished to rid themselves and the country of the hated presence of Gaveston. They claimed that, since Gaveston had 'disinherited the Crown' (i.e., become possessor of lands which ought to be part of the appanage of the Crown), and had alienated the King from his magnates, if those magnates demanded his removal the King was bound by the fourth clause of his oath to accept their demand.

At the April Parliament of 1308 a strong baronial group led by the old Earl of Lincoln, who had been one of the few lords to accept Gaveston's elevation to the earldom of Cornwall in a benign spirit, demanded Gaveston's immediate banishment. Lincoln was supported by the Earls of Lancaster, Warwick, Hereford, Pembroke and Surrey. Only the King's cousin Richmond and his nephew Gilbert de Clare of Gloucester did not join the opposition, but their attitude was by no means supportive of the King, it was merely neutral. Sir Hugh Despenser the elder, indeed, remained loyal to the King, but one supporter provided a very inadequate backing with which to resist so strong an opposition.

Nonetheless, the King at first appeared determined to defend Gaveston's position against the dubiously constitutional demand of the earls. Only when they appeared at Westminster in arms did the King at last capitulate and agree that Gaveston should forfeit his titles and be gone from England by 25 June. Archbishop Winchelsey, whom the King had recalled, and from whom he had no doubt expected grateful support, added his formidable influence to the opposition and pronounced a conditional excommunication upon Gaveston if he failed to leave by the agreed date or if he attempted to return.

Edward did what he could to mitigate the decline of Gaveston's fortunes. Castles and manors in England and Aquitaine were granted him, to support him in something like the position to which he had become accustomed; and he left the realm not as a disgraced exile but as the King's Lieutenant in Ireland. The King escorted him to Bristol and watched his departure, showing him honour to the last; but the fact remained that it had taken him less than a year to make himself intolerable to the nobility of England, and to affect most adversely the King's relations with them.

Edward II viewed a defeat exactly as his father had done: as a setback, to be recouped as speedily and effectively as possible. To the problem of securing Gaveston's recall from exile and reinstatement as Earl of Cornwall, Edward gave as much determination as his father would have given to mounting a new campaign against the Scots. It was unfortunate for his contemporary and posthumous reputation that the strength of will and the diplomatic ability which he displayed were not brought to bear upon the problems of government, but only upon a personal objective with which contemporary and later opinion was completely out of sympathy.

Imitating, no doubt, his father's dealings with the papacy, Edward wrote to the Pope requesting him to annul Archbishop Winchelsey's provisional excommunication of Gaveston. He then set to work upon the opposition and 'bent one after another to his will with gifts, promises and blandishments'.

Edward attempted to win over Archbishop Winchelsey himself by intervening on his behalf in a dispute between Winchelsey and the Florentine banker Amerigo dei Frescobaldi, concerning coinage rights. The King ordered Frescobaldi to give way, but Winchelsey, who was regarded by contemporaries as a second Becket, was not to be mollified by personal favours. The privileges of the Church were his concern, and at the time he was less interested in the King's problems than in those of Edward's old enemy Walter Langton, Bishop of

Coventry and Lichfield, who had been in prison since the beginning of the reign. The King was more successful in winning over some of his other opponents. Thomas of Lancaster was confirmed in his hereditary office of High Steward of England; Henry Percy, a powerful northern lord, received a grant of Scarborough Castle; and Queen Isabella received grants of Ponthieu and Montreuil. Isabella had not yet made her influence felt upon the English political scene; the grants were intended to win the support of her father who had been alienated by the insult offered to his daughter by the scandal of Edward's relations with Gaveston.

When Parliament met at Westminster in April 1309 Edward hoped that his appeasement policy would have borne fruit, but he found himself faced by an opposition party which demanded his consent to a complex programme of reforms, including the regulation of purveyance (i.e. the right of the Crown to obtain provisions at a fixed price), the limitation of the powers of royal officials and the reform of the Household. The King showed his obsessive state of mind by his counter-proposal that all reforms should be permitted in return for the recall and reinstatement of Gaveston. The lords refused this offer and Parliament was adjourned to Stamford, where a new session was to take place in July.

Before July, however, Edward had received a favourable answer from the Pope, and had managed to split the opposition by regaining the support of the Earls of Lincoln, Pembroke and Surrey. Gaveston was therefore recalled, Edward rode joyously to Chester to receive him, and they went together to the Parliament at Stamford. With Gaveston once more at his side, Edward was willing enough to accede to the demands of what remained of the opposition, that purveyance would be regulated and the Household reformed. It probably seemed to the King that he had got what he wanted and emerged relatively unscathed. His father had had to accept more serious limitations when he signed the Confirmation of the Charters, and had extricated himself in the end. Edward II doubtless expected to do the same.

As for Gaveston, his exile had been by no means inglorious. As the King's Lieutenant in Ireland he had aquitted himself well. The elegance of his household had set an example which

OPPOSITE Scarborough Castle photographed from the landward side. The castle is perched with apparent impregnability upon its headland on the Yorkshire coast.

61

the Irish were eager to imitate, his liberality had won him personal popularity, and he had proved himself an efficient soldier by quelling rebellion in Munster and Thomond. It was small wonder that he returned from Ireland with his arrogance undiminished. Nonetheless, he triumphed imprudently over his enemies, bestowing upon them mocking nicknames injurious to their pride and deflating to their dignity. The King may have laughed to hear the old, fat Earl of Lincoln nicknamed 'Burst-belly', the sallow Pembroke 'Joseph the Jew', Gloucester, whose mother had notoriously disliked her first husband, called 'The Cuckold's Bird', and Warwick 'The Black Dog of Arden'. But no-one else laughed, and baronial hatred of Gaveston was in no way diminished by the fact that he could unhorse his enemies in the lists as neatly as he could bestow a wounding insult.

By October, when the King summoned a council of his magnates to meet at York, Gaveston, by his insufferable pride and insolence, had reunited against himself the opposition which the King had successfully dismembered. The author of the *Vita Edwardi Secundi* penned a Latin couplet on Gaveston to this effect:

> Though handsome, rich and clever you may be
> Through insolence we may your ruin see.

At York the King received a disagreeable surprise when the Earls of Lancaster, Hereford, Warwick, Oxford and Arundel announced their refusal to attend the council because of Gaveston's presence.

The King and Gaveston spent Christmas together at Langley, and occupied themselves according to report 'in long-wished-for sessions of daily and intimate conversation'. It cannot be supposed that their conversation did not sometimes dwell upon the enmity with which they were surrounded.

In February 1310 when Parliament met at Westminster the King sent Gaveston to the north to ensure his personal safety, and went to Westminster accompanied by Gloucester, Richmond and Surrey to meet the recalcitrant lords. Supported by Winchelsey they presented to the King a long list of grievances and demanded that a commission should be set up empowered to implement all the reforms which they considered

OPPOSITE A fool or jester from the Windmill Psalter, *c.* 1300.
The Court Fool possessed the privilege of mocking king and nobility for the good of their souls and as an antidote to pride. Gaveston encroached upon the Fool's privilege without enjoying his immunity.

necessary. Edward could not do other than assent to the formation of the reform committee which gave itself the name of the Lords Ordainers.

The Lords Ordainers were twenty-one in number, and the committee was brought into being by a complex system of indirect election. The earls elected two bishops, and the bishops elected two earls; the chosen four elected two barons, and the resulting six co-opted fifteen more members. They attempted to be reasonably representative of all shades of political opinion. Among the bishops, the King's indomitable opponent Winchelsey was balanced by the moderate Langton of Chichester, the Chancellor. Among the earls, Gloucester and Richmond balanced the less amenable Hereford and Lancaster. Lincoln and Pembroke were both more interested in good government than in partisan measures.

The Lords Ordainers issued six preliminary Ordinances and then settled down to work out their reform programme at greater leisure. Edward immediately set to work to implement the policy which had proved successful before, that of breaking up the opposition. His first move was to leave Westminster, commanding the Chancellor 'with the Great Seal and all the

Chancery' to follow him wherever he went. This initial move was a failure, as Langton considered himself under obligation to remain with the committee, and therefore refused. Edward countered by dismissing Langton and appointing in his place Walter Reynolds who had been the treasurer of his household when he was Prince of Wales, and who was a personal friend upon whom Edward felt that he could rely. Shortly after appointing Reynolds his Chancellor, Edward obtained for him the bishopric of Worcester.

The King's next move was to announce a new campaign against the Scots. In September 1310, he went north, summoning the earls to follow him bringing their contingents. This move was also a failure, as only the Earls of Gloucester and Warwick consented to obey. Accordingly Edward embarked upon his campaign supported by only three earls, the two Ordainers who had consented to absent themselves from the committee, and by the Earl of Cornwall.

The campaign, directed by the King from Berwick, was neither a success nor a failure. The most active part in it was played by Gaveston, who marched north as far as Perth harrying the countryside. Gloucester led a similar expedition into Ettrick Forest, but the rest of the Ordainers, unimpressed, were not diverted from their task.

1311, an ill-omened year for the King, began unfortunately with the death of the Earl of Lincoln, whom Edward had appointed Regent while he was in Scotland. Not only was Lincoln a loss as a moderating influence upon the Ordainers, his death led to the inheritance of his two earldoms of Lincoln and Salisbury by his son-in-law Thomas, Earl of Lancaster. As Lancaster was also Earl of Leicester and Derby, a total of five earldoms made him far and away the greatest of the magnates. Wealth and territorial greatness lifted him to the leadership of the opposition, and the intensity of his hatred for Gaveston gave his leadership an aspect of bitterness that was bound to be destructive in its influence.

Early in 1311 Lancaster, who owed the King homage for his new earldoms, went north to do his duty, but he immediately showed his hand by refusing to do his homage in Scotland. Edward, in a conciliatory spirit, came south of the Border to meet him at Haggerston Castle, but Lancaster was determined

OPPOSITE The gilt-bronze effigy of Eleanor of Castile, made by William Torel in Westminster Abbey. A controversy exists as to whether this is an idealised portrait or a conventional image of a queen. The top of the tomb is decorated with heraldic lions for Laon, and castles for Castile.

64

to make his point, and at the ceremony he refused to greet Gaveston, who as ever was at the King's side. Edward was well aware of the implications of Lancaster's behaviour, and when he went south in July to attend Parliament, he left Gaveston safely housed in the castle of Bamburgh, on the coast of Northumberland.

In the knowledge that, though Gaveston was the principal target of the Lords Ordainers' enmity, the reform committee required that many other grievances be dealt with, Edward made a desperate effort to win the only victory that he cared about by agreeing to accept any of the Ordinances which concerned himself on condition that Gaveston was unharmed and his position unaffected. The Lords Ordainers unceremoniously refused.

The Ordinances were set out in forty-one articles. Though the theme of misgovernment and the misleading of the King by evil counsel occurs again and again throughout the Ordinances, it was the twentieth article which specifically declared that Piers of Gaveston had 'misled and ill-advised our lord the King, and enticed him to do evil in various deceitful ways', and decreed that Gaveston 'as an open enemy of the King and his people, shall be altogether exiled from England, Scotland, Ireland and Wales, and from all the dominion of our lord the King, both on this side and the other side of the sea'.

It is significant that the author of the *Vita Edwardi Secundi* in his account of the Ordinances transcribed in full only the article which referred to Gaveston and his misdeeds, as being the one which was of the greatest public interest. Nonetheless, Gaveston was not the only individual to whom the Lords Ordainers took exception, neither were his misdeeds the only ones to be condemned. Also to be exiled were Henry de Beaumont, a maternal cousin of the King, and his sister Isabella de Vescy, the custodian of Gaveston's refuge, Bamburgh Castle.

A more important object of the Lords Ordainers' disapproval was the banker Amerigo dei Frescobaldi. Not only was he the greatest of the King's creditors, suspect as a too-influential foreigner, but the loans which the King was able to raise from him and other financiers gave the Crown a certain amount of financial independence which the magnates saw as a threat to their own influence. Furthermore, Frescobaldi held the post of

66

Bamburgh Castle, Gaveston's refuge on the coast of Northumberland.

pres le tres pas
du bon roy edou
ard regna sire
edouard son filz
lequel nasqui
en canarenan.

solempnuellement con
monstier par lartheues
de bbincestre et de cant
presse fut si grande qu
de dalbuelle fut murt
place. Et puis si tost q
duard de canarenan

Constable of Bordeaux, which gave him in appearance at least a dubious connection with the family of Gaveston's mother, the Calhau, a family of Gascon nobility who engaged with considerable success in international finance. That one of the Calhau was Mayor of Bordeaux, and that Gaveston was in the habit of banking the vast sums of money which he received from the King with both the Calhau and the Frescobaldi was quite sufficient to convince the Lords Ordainers that Amerigo dei Frescobaldi, along with Gaveston and the other undesirables, must go.

However, the concomitant of his removal was a programme of financial reform intended to oblige and enable the King to live without recourse to foreign credit. Alienations of Crown lands and any other forms of gift were not to be made until the King's debts had been paid. The issue of the customs and other royal revenues were to be paid direct to the Exchequer, from which an allowance was to be made for the maintenance of the King's Household, so that he could 'live of his own without recourse to *prises* other than those due and accustomed'. A *prise* was simply 'the taking of something for the use of the King by virtue of the royal prerogative'. The Ordinances decreed that in future there were to be no *prises* of corn, merchandise or other goods, whether in the form of purveyance or otherwise, without the consent of the owner and without proper payment. At the same time, they decreed that new customs levied since the coronation of Edward I were to be abolished.

In the financial Ordinances, however, the Lords Ordainers had attempted to solve economic problems with which they were not qualified to deal, for 'by forbidding increases in the customs while at the same time cutting off the supply of foreign credit, the Ordainers were making the solution of the financial problem impossible'.

From financial measures the Lord Ordainers proceeded to administrative reform. The King's power to appoint officials was to be restricted in future, and the appointment of all the high officers of state and of the King's Household was to require the consent of the magnates in Parliament. Upon appointment, all officials were to take an oath to maintain the Ordinances. Abuses in the administration of the law were to be remedied;

OPPOSITE The marriage of Edward II to Isabella, daughter of Philippe IV, at the Church of Notre Dame, Boulogne.

69

for example, in future the King was not to enjoy the right of issuing charters of protection or of pardon to known male-factors, nor were litigants to be permitted to produce letters from the King to excuse non-appearance in court. These measures suggest that the King either had been, or was considered to have been, guilty of showing favour with remarkable irresponsibility.

Finally the Lords Ordainers claimed for themselves the right of interpreting any doubtful points in Magna Carta and the Charter of the Forest, and decreed that all statutes should be maintained conditionally upon their infringing neither these two Charters nor the Ordinances. The Ordinances were to be maintained in every particular, and as a further guarantee of good government Parliament was to be held once or if necessary twice a year, and at each Parliament a committee of lords should be elected to hear any grievances which should be raised against the King's ministers.

The Ordinances have been the subject of much learned argument, and many differing opinions have been held by historians concerning both their significance and the actual aims of the Lords Ordainers. Basically, however, it seems that in spite of envy and personal hatred of Gaveston, the Lords Ordainers were genuinely desirous of ridding the country of the presence of a man who engrossed the King's attention to the exclusion of all else, including the actual business of government. At the same time, though the Ordainers appear to have been genuine in their concern that the realm should be well governed, their concept of good government was one in which they themselves played an influential part, and they were concerned to conserve all those privileges which enabled them to do so. Finally, though they wished to publicise their public-spiritedness as much as possible, and by so doing to gain popular support, this did not entail any desire 'to broaden the basis of the constitution or to alter the structure of government'. In other words, the aims of the Lords Ordainers were oligarchic, and it would be a mistake to impute to them any desire to limit the power of the monarch in the interests of promoting ideals of democracy, which they did not possess.

Edward's own view of the Ordinances was summed up by his remark that they organised his life 'as one would provide

70

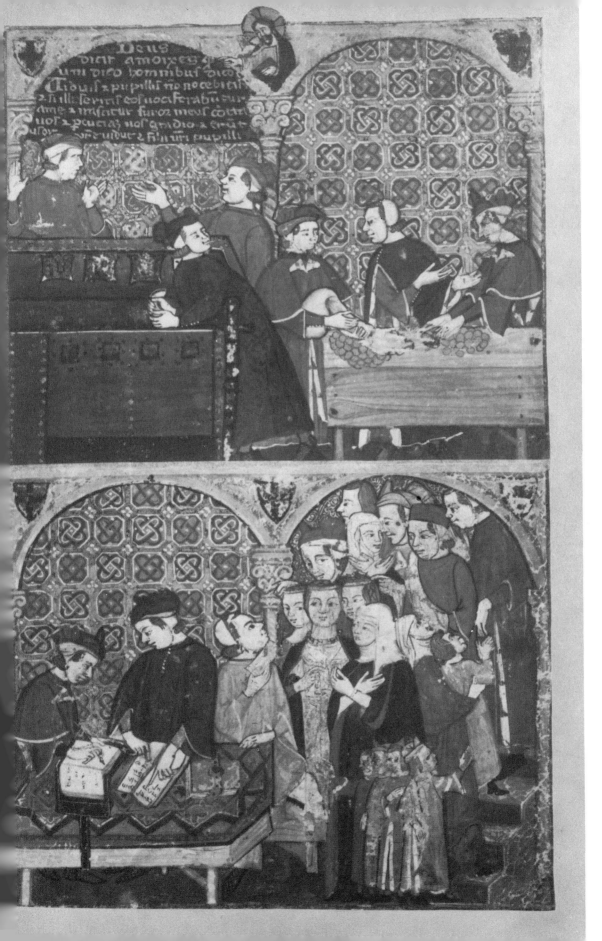

for an idiot'. His initial anger was justifiable enough from his own viewpoint, but it was not long before he realised that even if he could not prevent the promulgation of the Ordinances, he could hinder their implementation almost endlessly. Indeed, much of the rest of the reign could be described in terms of a struggle over the implementation of the Ordinances.

However, the King could not evade the decree which was the most public issue at stake: the exile of Gaveston. It was made clear to Edward that the outcome of his refusal to submit would be civil war. The Ordinances were publicly proclaimed at Paul's Cross on 27 September 1311; Gaveston was to be out of the country, stripped of his titles and condemned to perpetual exile, by 1 November. In the interim he remained with the King, and in the event it was 3 November before he departed.

Gaveston went, but he did not go far and he did not go for long. Probably he went to Flanders, but before the end of the month he was rumoured to be back in England, 'now in the King's apartments, now at Wallingford and now at Tintagel Castle'. Possibly he persuaded the King that the best way of evading the Ordinances was to ignore them, for, with the approach of the Christmas season, all pretence at secrecy was abandoned; the King held his Christmas Court at Windsor, and Gaveston appeared openly at his side.

His insouciance and effrontery were rewarded with immediate excommunication by the redoubtable Winchelsey; and, while Edward bestowed upon his favourite the earldom of Cornwall for the third time, the lords prepared for civil war.

At this point, even the King's nephew Gloucester was prepared to fight against him, and with the other earls he took an oath to defend the Ordinances. It was agreed that the earls should organise local tournaments which would provide reasons for armed gatherings while keeping secret their real intentions until the last moment. But Edward did not remain in ignorance for long. Early in 1312 he and Gaveston made for the north, intending to negotiate with Robert the Bruce for Gaveston's safety to be guaranteed in Scotland. Robert the Bruce declined to guarantee it, and the King and Gaveston were left stranded in Newcastle, threatened by the approach of Thomas of Lancaster.

Edward and Gaveston were as unwilling to be besieged as

Newcastle was unwilling to defend them. They fled to Tynemouth and thence, even more ignominiously, took boat to Scarborough, leaving behind them their households, baggage train, arms and treasure. Among all the impedimenta was the unfortunate Queen Isabella, doubly humiliated first by being dragged around the country in the wake of her husband and his favourite and then by being abandoned. No doubt her situation was made all the worse by the fact that the King had not neglected his dynastic duty; she was three months pregnant. At Tynemouth, Isabella was captured, though in effect rescued, by Thomas of Lancaster, who comforted her with a promise that he would not rest until he had separated the King and Gaveston.

By the time that Lancaster next heard of them, however, Edward and Gaveston had separated by mutual consent. Gaveston took refuge in the castle of Scarborough, perched seemingly impregnably on its cliff, while the King went to York, presumably with the intention of gathering reinforcements to resist the earls. Since it had not been necessary for Lancaster to part Edward and Gaveston forcibly, he took it upon himself at least to ensure that they did not rejoin each other. While Lancaster with his forces stationed himself midway between Scarborough and York, the Earls of Pembroke and Surrey, aided by Henry Percy, laid siege to Scarborough Castle.

Gaveston had entered Scarborough in haste and found it ill-provisioned. At the end of a fortnight, he was obliged to come to terms with the besiegers. It was agreed that he should surrender upon the assurance of his personal safety, and that he should present himself before Parliament which should decide his future. His retainers were to be permitted to remain in occupation of Scarborough until August, and were to be free to revictual it; and if, by that time, his future had not been decided, he was to be permitted to return to Scarborough. These terms were so remarkably generous that one chronicler put on record the suspicion that Pembroke, who offered the terms, had been bribed by the King. This, however, turned out not to be the case; the terms were suggested purely by Pembroke's magnanimity. On 19 May 1312, Gaveston surrendered to Pembroke, Surrey and Percy, who on their side swore upon the Host that they would abide faithfully by the surrender terms.

The Art of Jousting

In the fourteenth century jousting was a sport in which
knights were frequently maimed and sometimes killed;
it was scarcely less dangerous than the warfare for which
it was intended to provide training and practice.

RIGHT A knight strikes another on the helm from
the misericord at Gloucester Cathedral. Points were
scored for hits on the helm and shield as well as for
unhorsing the opponent.

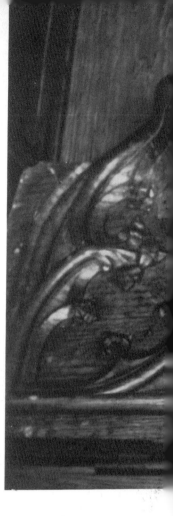

BELOW RIGHT A caparisoned knight receives his helmet
from a lady. Jousting was part of the drama of courtly
love and knights frequently wore a scarf or ribbon
in token of a lady's favour.
BELOW Jousting knights from Gregory's Decretals of
the early fourteenth century. The trumpeters gave
the signal for the start of each course.

It was an unhappy thing for Gaveston that Pembroke, being a man of honour himself, expected to find a similar honour in others. He took it upon himself to escort Gaveston to his own castle of Wallingford, where he could remain in custody until the opening of Parliament. A leisurely southward journey had brought them to the village of Deddington, ten miles south of Banbury, by the evening of 9 June. Here Pembroke, naturally wishing to spend the night with his wife who was only a few miles away at his manor of Bampton, left his prisoner, without the least suspicion that the more rancorous of the earls might take the law into their own hands. Warwick, for one, was fully prepared to do so. Early in the morning on 10 June, he brought an armed force to surround Deddington rectory, in which Gaveston had been lodged, and entered the house to wake him with the words, 'Get up, traitor, you are taken!'

Gaveston was not permitted to prepare himself for his fate with any dignity, but was hustled barefoot out of the house and forced to walk with his captors towards the town of Warwick. Eventually, after they had brought him some miles, they relented of their rough treatment sufficiently to mount him on a mare, in the interests of haste. At Warwick, a crowd inevitably materialised to jeer, and to see him led into the castle, where he was unceremoniously thrown into a dungeon.

Pembroke, on his return to Deddington was enraged, not because he had any tender feelings towards Gaveston, but because he had taken an oath to protect him and had pledged both his honour and his lands upon it. He attempted first to persuade Gloucester to help him induce Warwick to relinquish the prisoner, and when Gloucester was unco-operative he appealed to the University and burgesses of Oxford to lend their influence. None, however, was willing to intervene on behalf of the detested Gaveston, and Pembroke was obliged to stand by impotently while events ran their course.

The Earl of Warwick was joined at Warwick Castle by the Earls of Lancaster, Hereford and Arundel. Warwick, when he had heard that Gaveston had given him the nickname of 'The Black Dog of Arden', had remarked that if Gaveston called him a dog he would justify the name by biting him at the first opportunity. But now that the opportunity had arisen, Warwick did not show himself very eager to bestow the bite.

76

The four earls were agreed that Gaveston must pay the penalty for his misdeeds, yet Warwick stood aside while Lancaster assumed responsibility for exacting the penalty.

Inevitably, the earls decided that Gaveston must die, but since he was Earl of Cornwall, whether they approved the fact or not, and since he was Gloucester's brother-in-law and the husband of the King's niece, they agreed that he should die as a nobleman, by beheading. Accordingly, on 19 June they brought him out of his dungeon and marched him to Blacklow Hill, two miles from Warwick and within the estates of Thomas of Lancaster. There, while Warwick lurked in his castle, and Lancaster, Hereford and Arundel watched from a distance, Gaveston was beheaded. His head was presented to Lancaster, who was thus irrevocably marked as the man responsible for the deed.

The earls returned whence they came, leaving the headless corpse where it lay. Its subsequent fate was macabre in the extreme. Four cobblers took it up and carried it on a ladder to the Earl of Warwick who refused to receive it. Therefore, with strange solicitude, they seamed the head back upon the body and carried it to the Dominicans of Oxford, who received and embalmed it, but kept it unburied since Gaveston had died under Archbishop Winchelsey's excommunication.

So ended the brave and insouciant young man for whose sake the King had been willing to incur the enmity of all the magnates of his realm, the very men whose loyalty and co-operation it behoved him to secure if he aspired to rule with any success at all.

As for Gaveston himself, it is difficult to see wherein his misdeeds actually merited death; essentially he paid the penalty for the King's misdeeds rather than his own. No doubt he was personally infuriating to the point of intolerability, and arguably no doubt he could be condemned as the instigator of the King's follies. Certainly this was the view taken by the Lords Ordainers when they castigated him as having 'misled and ill-advised our lord the King, and enticed him to do evil in various deceitful ways'.

The magnates of England professed to detest Gaveston as an upstart and a foreigner. However, he was nobly born and might have held high office in the state without comment if his

The beheaded Gaveston
beneath the feet of
Guy Beauchamp, Earl of
Warwick, from the
Rous Roll.

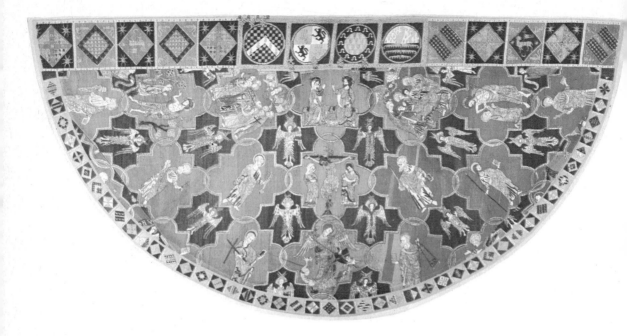

ABOVE The Syon Cope, an embroidery work c. 1300, shows scenes from the New Testament.

LEFT A detail of the Ascension panel of the retable in Norwich Cathedral.

rise had been sufficiently gradual; he was made to appear an upstart by the instantaneousness of his advancement and the prodigality of the King's favour. As for his foreignness, being a Gascon he was born an English subject, and he was probably not noticeably more foreign than most of the Norman-French-speaking nobility of England. These professed reasons for hating him have the appearance of excuses rather than realities. Undoubtedly, envy at his good fortune, hatred aroused by his arrogance, and disgust at the King's unconcealed infatuation with him were the causes of the brutal scene on Blacklow Hill.

The King was stunned by the news of his death. Grief and shock do not lead to eloquence, and it must have been from such a state of mind that the King produced the words 'By God's Soul, he acted as a fool. If he had taken my advice he would never have fallen into the hands of the earls.' Those who had expected to hear a flood of lamentation ridiculed the King's few words, but subsequently he found his tongue and lamented bitterly. Edward's contemporary biographer commented: 'In the lament of David upon Jonathan love is depicted which is said to have surpassed the love of women. Our King also spoke thus; and further he planned to avenge the death of Piers.'

For the time being, however, he was in no position to do so, since he had made his own situation so precariously isolated. But, with the death of Gaveston, the immediate pretext for civil war was removed. The magnates had no further wish to fight the King, yet a settlement between King and magnates was by no means easy. Gaveston's death had split the party which had been united upon the question of the Ordinances. Pembroke and Surrey, linked by the oath which they had taken to safe-guard Gaveston until he should appear before Parliament, now gave their support to the King. Lancaster, Hereford, Arundel and Warwick, held together by the crime they had committed, attempted to justify themselves on the grounds that by the authority of the Ordinances, Gaveston was a traitor who could lawfully be summarily executed. The King had in fact revoked the Ordinances at the time of Gaveston's death, though the earls pleaded that they were in ignorance of this. According to one account of Gaveston's execution, the earls had gone to the trouble of finding two justices to pronounce sentence before taking him to Blacklow Hill. Nonetheless, whether Gaveston's

A knight receives his sword from a king. The ceremony of knighthood possessed an awesome and quasi-religious solemnity.

death was summary execution, judicial murder or merely a brutal killing, the fact remained that the four earls had dishonoured the oath of their confederates Pembroke and Surrey in a manner for which there was no extenuating argument. The inexcusability of their behaviour considerably strengthened the King's position.

Edward sent Pembroke to France with a request for assistance from Philip IV, who responded by sending his brother Prince Louis of Evreux to mediate between Edward and the earls. Assisted by two papal emissaries, Louis of Evreux spent many months working to achieve a settlement.

In the meantime, Queen Isabella gave birth to the child with which she had been pregnant when Edward and Gaveston

abandoned her at Newcastle. The child, born on 13 November 1312, was a son, the future King Edward III. His birth was the occasion of great public rejoicing, and the King himself found pleasure in the birth of an heir which lifted his spirits a little from the misery of Gaveston's death.

From this point, the relationship of Edward and his Queen underwent considerable improvement. She had naturally hated Gaveston, and no doubt her life seemed a great deal pleasanter without him. As for the King, he showed the quality of the love that he had had for Gaveston by not replacing him with a new favourite. Edward had been enslaved to an individual not to a sexual habit. Perhaps for this reason, Isabella was able to establish a better relationship with her husband. It may be doubted, in view of the end of the story of their marriage, whether there was ever much affection between them; but at least it was not a story of mutual hatred from beginning to end.

In the spring of 1313 Edward and his Queen went together to France to attend the knighting of Isabella's three brothers, and in July they returned, in time for Edward to give his attention to the final stages of the negotiations presided over by Louis of Evreux.

Edward's position had been further improved by the death of Archbishop Winchelsey in the spring. In his place Edward had managed to secure the appointment of his old friend Walter Reynolds as Archbishop of Canterbury. Reynolds was not a strong character, and the change of primate should perhaps be expressed in terms of the loss to the opposition rather than the gain to the King. Winchelsey had been ill for many months, but the removal of even the shadow of his influence doubtless brought the settlement nearer.

Two issues in particular had deferred it for so long: the first had been the fate of Gaveston's possessions captured at Newcastle by Thomas of Lancaster, and the second and more serious issue had been whether or not the earls would admit themselves to have been guilty over Gaveston's death.

The question of Gaveston's possessions developed into a long, contentious wrangle, because they included many valuable jewels presented to Gaveston by the King. Among them were a golden torque set with a great ruby called 'the Cherry', a gold ring set with a sapphire, said to have been made by St Dunstan,

a belt decorated with cameos set in gold, valued at £166 13s. 4d., and an enormous uncut ruby valued at £1,000, which Gaveston had not left at Newcastle, but carried around with him. It had been found concealed about his person after he was dead. Considering the value of these jewels, it was small wonder that the King wished to regain them, not merely for reasons of sentiment. After prolonged negotiation Thomas of Lancaster agreed to restore them.

The question of the earls' guilt presented a greater problem. The earls were reluctant to acknowledge their guilt both on principle and because of the possibility of future danger to themselves if the King should ever gain a position of unfettered power. Edward, on his side, flatly refused to admit the earls not guilty and thus brand Gaveston a traitor. In the end, the dead-lock was broken by the suggestion that the earls should admit their fault and offer the King their humble apology, in return for which Edward should grant a general pardon to them and to their followers. Edward agreed, and undoubtedly he had the best of the bargain, because in the final settlement no reference at all was made to the Ordinances, but the implication of their invalidity was carried in the earls' apology for the slaying of Gaveston.

Apology and pardon were exchanged in Westminster Hall on 14 October 1313, and the settlement was celebrated by two banquets, one given by the King and the other by Thomas of Lancaster. Certainly the memory of the troubles of the past few years could not be washed away in the wine which flowed at those two banquets. The best that can be said is that Edward had gained a respite. Perhaps, if from this point he had been both adroit and fortunate, the troubled beginning of his reign might have passed into oblivion.

A contemporary comment concerning this moment of his reign did not waste words upon the past, but it was terse and to the point: 'He has achieved nothing laudable or memorable, save that he was married royally and has begotten an heir to his Crown.'

OPPOSITE Westminster Hall, where the King and Lancaster gave banquets to celebrate their temporary peace.

3
Scotland
1314

Maids of England, sore may you mourn
For your lemans you have lost at Bannocksbourn
    With a heave and a ho!
What weeneth the King of England
So soon to have won Scotland
    With a rombelow!

(Contemporary Scottish song, adapted by
Christopher Marlowe in *Edward II*)

WHILE EDWARD II had struggled to retain his beloved Gaveston, and the earls had retaliated first by endeavouring to enforce the Ordinances and then by slaughtering the favourite, Robert the Bruce had profited by the disorder in England and made good use of the time by consolidating his position in Scotland.

After his victory at Loudon Hill, Robert the Bruce was still far from enjoying universal recognition as King of Scots even in Scotland itself. The kindred of the murdered Comyn were resolutely inimical to him, and some hard fighting took place before they were brought to heel. However, his successes against them gained him increasing respect and support. In 1309 the Scottish Parliament was summoned to St Andrews to give him formal recognition, and in 1310 the Scottish clergy defied the papal excommunication by declaring in his favour.

The English occupying forces left in Scotland by Edward I and sorely neglected by Edward II still held out, defending the east coast towns and the strongest fortresses in the south-east of the country. In 1310 the grip of the occupation was still strong enough to make life very difficult for the people of the east and the lowlands who naturally did not wish to jeopardise their lives and livelihoods by supporting the losing side. The Lanercost Chronicle vividly describes their plight, and their basic sympathies:

> The Scots were so divided among themselves that sometimes the father was with the Scottish side and the son the English, and *vice versa*; also one brother might be with the Scots and another with the English; yea, even the same individual be first with one party and then with the other. But all those who were with the English were merely feigning, either because it was the stronger party, or in order to save the lands they possessed in England; for their hearts were always with their own people, although their persons might not be so.

The ineffectiveness of Edward II's single expedition to Scotland in 1310–11 served, however, to illustrate the erosion of English power in Scotland, and after Edward's withdrawal Robert the Bruce was able to adopt a much more aggressive policy. With patience and determination he set about the reduction of the towns and fortresses which remained in English hands.

PREVIOUS PAGES Casts of the great seal (left) and the signet of Robert I, King of Scots.

88

The King of Scots possessed no siege engines, and the story of his success is largely a story of brilliant surprise attacks carried out by night with no greater resources than light scaling-ladders put to good use by his commandos. He regained Linlithgow in 1311, surprise failed at Berwick, but early in 1313, he recovered Perth, Dundee, Edinburgh and Roxburgh.

At the same time, Robert the Bruce financed his war effort by a series of devastating raids into England which swiftly convinced the men of the northern counties that it was wiser to pay a high price for a short truce than to have their crops and cattle seized and their homes burned over their heads. In 1311, after the Scots had burned the town of Corbridge, the county of Northumberland offered £2,000 for a truce. It has been estimated that King Robert may have gained as much as £20,000 in the 'blackmail' paid to him by towns, abbeys and local communities. It enabled him to purchase from the Low Countries and the Hanseatic ports armour and weapons which were not manufactured in Scotland. By the time Gaveston was dead and Edward had reached his uneasy settlement with his opponents, the position of Robert the Bruce was very different from what it had been when Edward was last in Scotland.

In 1313 Berwick still remained in English hands, and so did the great fortress of Stirling, which was being besieged by King Robert's brother, Edward Bruce. That a full-scale siege could now be undertaken is in itself illustrative of the changed situation. At midsummer 1313 the governor of Stirling Castle, Sir Philip Mowbray, made terms with Edward Bruce, by which it was agreed that if an English relieving army failed to come within three leagues of Stirling by midsummer 1314, Mowbray would surrender. This agreement between besieger and besieged, made without consulting either the King of England or the King of Scots, committed both sovereigns to the confrontation which they had hitherto avoided.

King Robert was justifiably angered by his brother's action. So far he had relied upon guerilla warfare, and his successes had amply vindicated his methods. *Good King Robert's Testament* records in rhyme the fact that the Scottish King had greater confidence in a policy of scorched earth and of

> Wiles and wakening in the night
> And mickle noises made on height

Medieval Crafts

Edward took great enjoyment in the company of the common people, working with them at rustic crafts such as thatching and shoeing horses. This scandalised his nobles who considered such work beneath the dignity of a king.

RIGHT A blacksmith beats out a horseshoe.
BELOW A man carrying loaves of bread stops to talk to a woman at the spinning wheel.
BOTTOM A carpenter and his mate.

tuam domine requiram·
Ne auertas faciem tuam
a me· ne declines in ira a
seruo tuo·
Adiutor meus esto domine
ne derelinquas me· nec
despicias me deus salutaris
meus
Qm pr meus z mat ma
dereliquerunt me· dns au
tem assumpsit me·
Legem pone michi dne
in uia tua· dirige me in

ce epo umm apo xxri. i·fr no mum t aremum te pælaone
no non est plvitmn. f evamb; ca ma lu no rves uls muns.

A messenger brings a
letter to a king.

than in pitched battle with an enemy whose resources in
manpower, armaments and supplies were infinitely greater
than his own. Nonetheless, since it appeared that his brother had
committed him to do battle, he prepared resolutely for the
contest which could cost him his crown or consolidate his
position beyond further challenge.

Sir Philip Mowbray, when he had made his arrangement
with Edward Bruce, was chivalrously permitted to go south to
explain the position to Edward II. To the English King the
arrangement seemed very much more acceptable than it did
to the King of Scots. Indeed, Edward may even have regarded
it as something of a godsend. A new campaign in Scotland was
the most likely means at his disposal of gaining him the support
of his opponents; and should he defeat Robert the Bruce in
battle, the resulting prestige would make past troubles seem
relatively insignificant. Anticipating this desirable outcome,
Edward prepared for war with confidence and enthusiasm.

On 23 December 1313, Edward sent out writs to his magnates
summoning them to appear in arms with their contingents at
Berwick on 10 June 1314. Plenty of time was allowed for
military preparations, little for the relieving operation itself.

It must have been a blow to Edward's initial optimism when
four of the earls, Lancaster, Warwick, Surrey and Arundel,
refused the summons. The reason given was that according to

92

the Ordinances the King should have obtained the consent of the magnates in Parliament before making war. It was an insincere excuse, to cover personal animosity and disloyalty to the King, considering in the first place that Edward and the earls had recently been formally reconciled without reference made to the Ordinances, and in the second place that Edward had previously been criticised for his lack of enthusiasm for the conquest of Scotland. However, the four earls could not avoid sending contingents to fight for the King in accordance with their feudal obligations, though each of them sent the minimal quota. From the rest of his subjects, Edward's summons to war won an enthusiastic response.

The Earls of Gloucester, Pembroke and Hereford at once prepared to accompany the King in person, and he was well supplied with seasoned soldiers, some of whom had gained their experience abroad, some of whom were veterans of his father's wars in Wales and Scotland. Sir Henry de Beaumont and Sir Hugh Despenser the elder, though unpopular with some of the earls as intimate and uncritical friends of the King, were both good soldiers. Sir Hugh Despenser's son and namesake, a highly intelligent young man who had played quite a prominent part in the preparation of the Ordinances, but who had recently aligned himself with his father as a King's man, was also a great asset to Edward, both in his military capacity and as a loyal servant and adviser, not only on the campaign of 1314 but also in the years that followed. Indeed, as time passed, he became more and more closely associated with the King in service and in friendship.

Among the veterans of Edward I's Welsh and Scottish campaigns were Sir Ralph de Monthermer, Sir Robert Clifford and Sir Maurice de Berkeley, Sir Pain Tiptoft, Sir Marmaduke Tweng and Sir Giles D'Argentan, the last of whom was described by John Barbour as the third best knight of his day, though Barbour omitted to name the best and second best. Edward II, ever generous in such matters, had taken great pains to secure D'Argentan's release from imprisonment in Salonika in time to permit his participation in the Scottish campaign. Also serving in Edward's army were Sir Ingram de Umfraville, a Norman-Scot who still held to his English allegiance, and John Comyn, the son of King Robert's murdered rival. There

OVERLEAF Scotland and the North of England in the fourteenth century. Hadrian's Wall marks the border country which was the scene of continual raid and pillage from both sides. (Bodleian MS Gough gen. top. 16)

93

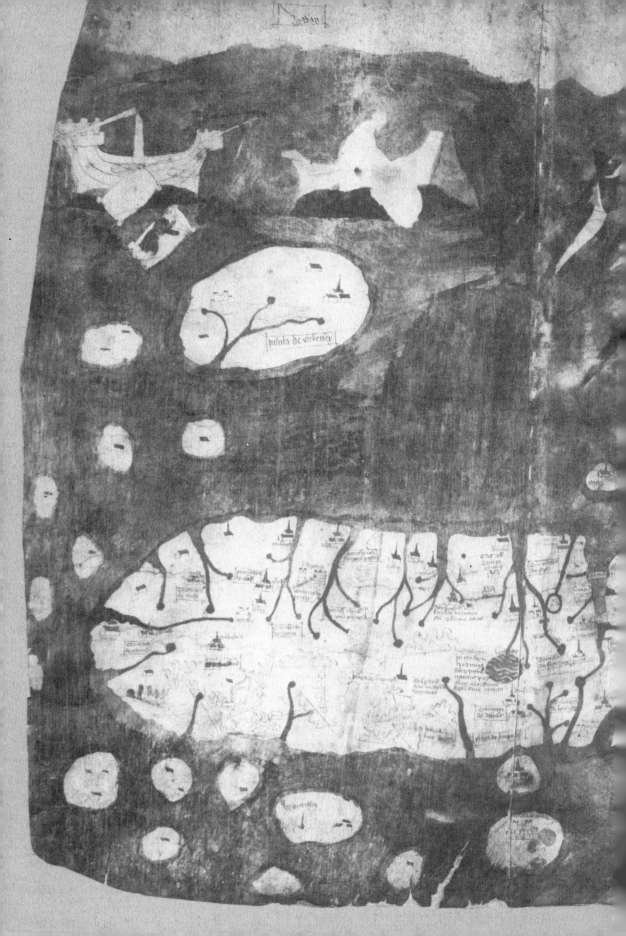

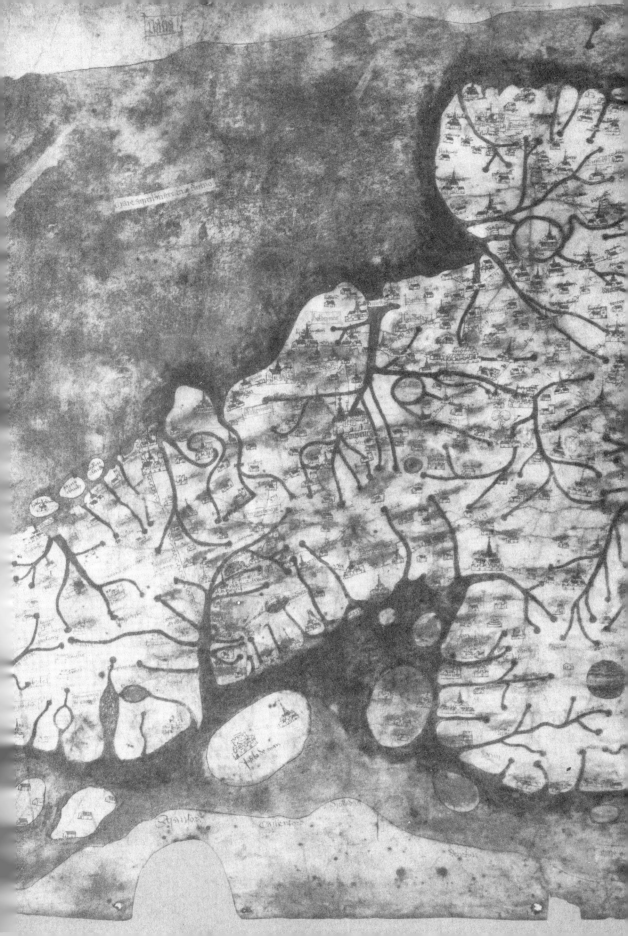

Robert I, King of Scots,
as portrayed on his
great seal.

were Welsh, Irish and Gascon contingents, and a few adventurous foreigners from Flanders and Germany.

The actual numbers of Edward's army have been the subject of much controversy. But leaving out the most sanguine and the most conservative estimates, the probability and the consensus of learned opinion puts the total at about 2,500 cavalry and 15,000 infantry. Robert the Bruce awaited him with an army numbering between 7,000 and 10,000, which included only a small force of light cavalry, numbering no more than 500. All King Robert's generalship and superior knowledge of the terrain would be required to counterbalance that alarming difference in numbers.

The Scots, however, had certain advantages, which John Barbour enumerated in a speech which he put into the mouth of King Robert himself. Their war of independence had given the Scots a strong sense of their national identity and of the righteousness of their cause; they could have confidence in the approval of God, the King is made to say, and may well have said, and they could derive strength from the fact that

> ... for our lives
> And for our children and our wives,
> And for our freedom and our land
> In battle we are forced to stand.

Whereas the English

> ... have come thus far
> For naught but to increase their power.

Nonetheless, for Edward II a very great deal was at stake, and even if he could not, like King Robert, encourage his followers with an inspiring cause, he could at least arouse their enthusiasm with the happy prospect of the rewards of success. Indeed, as Barbour rather humorously put it,

> ... liberally among his men
> He dealt the land of Scotland then.
> He showed great generosity
> With other people's property.

When Edward reached Berwick, he bestowed upon Hugh Despenser the younger the lands of King Robert's supporter Thomas Randolph, Earl of Moray, among other prospective

RIGHT The seal of Robert
Fitzwalter shows the
style of armour at
the beginning of the
fourteenth century.

BELOW Naval combat
illustrated in Gregory's
Decretals.

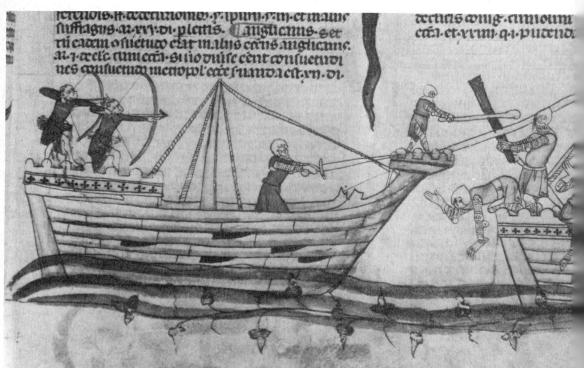

grants. It was evident that King Edward hoped for greater things than the relief of Stirling Castle.

Time, however, was running very short for the avowed purpose of the expedition when Edward left Berwick on 17 June; yet he left in high spirits, more like a man going joyously on a pilgrimage to Compostella, said the author of the *Vita Edwardi Secundi*, than a King going to war. His army, with its huge baggage-train, marched up Lauderdale towards Edinburgh, which was reached on 21 June. Long forced marches would be required if Stirling were to be reached by Midsummer Day. A march of over twenty miles brought the English army to Falkirk, and another march of similar length on the following day brought it within striking distance of Stirling and within sight of the enemy.

The Roman road from Falkirk to Stirling passed first through the Torwood, an area adequately described by its old Gaelic name *coille torr*, 'the wood of rocky outcrops', and thence through the more heavily wooded New Park, an area enclosed by Alexander III for hunting, and given its name to distinguish it from the older hunting preserve, the King's Park, near the foot of the rock of Stirling Castle.

As King Edward's army marched from Falkirk, King Robert awaited his approach in the Torwood, but thence he withdrew to the better cover and the stronger position of the New Park. Between the Torwood and the New Park, the route was intersected by the Bannock Burn, one of the many streams which flowed across the low-lying Carse of Stirling to join the River Forth in its convoluted course past Stirling towards the sea. The Carse of Stirling was then known as 'The Pows' or 'Les Polles', denoting an area of muddy streams, which is worth mentioning as the muddiness of the area lent its essential character to the conflict which took place there.

Having established himself in the New Park, King Robert did what he could to hinder the English advance by ordering 'pottes', or pits, disguised with branches and grass, to be dug on either side of the road north of the Bannock Burn and south of the New Park. Professor G. W. S. Barrow, in his study of Robert the Bruce, has described the 'pottes' as the medieval equivalent of a mine-field, 'designed not only to cause casualties . . . but to force the enemy to bunch at a single well-guarded

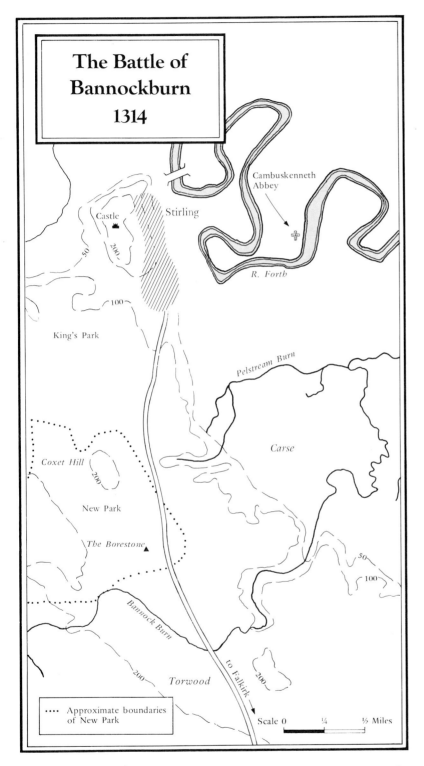

The Battle of
Bannockburn
1314

Cambuskenneth
Abbey

Stirling

Castle

50

200

R. Forth

100

King's Park

Pelstream Burn

Coxet Hill

200

Carse

New Park

The Borestone

50

100

Bannock Burn

to Falkirk

200

200

Torwood

···· Approximate boundaries
of New Park

Scale 0   ¼   ½ Miles

spot'. It appears that the 'pottes' admirably served their intended purpose.

When the English army reached the Torwood a quarrel broke out among the leaders. Edward had appointed the Earl of Gloucester as Constable, an office which gave him command of the vanguard of the army. The Earl of Hereford claimed that as Hereditary Constable of England it was automatically his right to have that command. Edward, who had evidently overlooked this problem, settled the quarrel by appointing them joint commanders, a solution in the interests more of dignity than of efficiency.

No sooner had this problem been solved than Sir Philip Mowbray, doubtless permitted to leave Stirling under safe conduct from King Robert, appeared to inform King Edward that he was now within three leagues of Stirling Castle, and since honour was technically satisfied, he, Mowbray, need not surrender, nor Edward give battle if he chose not to do so. But the English, though weary, were too confident of victory to contemplate not giving battle. Mowbray therefore retired, and the English vanguard pressed on towards the New Park.

It was here that an incident occurred which somewhat lowered the morale of the English, and commensurably raised that of the Scots.

On the outskirts of the New Park, the English had their first glimpse of the enemy, a group of horsemen one of whom wore a Crown of Ornament on his helmet. The Earl of Hereford's nephew, Sir Henry de Bohun, was the first to realise that they had come upon the King of Scots making a tour of inspection. Seeing the possibility of a deed which would amount to winning the victory at a single blow, Sir Henry set his lance at rest and charged. But in Barbour's expressive line, 'Sir Henry missed the noble King.' And as he passed, Robert the Bruce, who as fortune would have it had a battle-axe in his hand, rose in his stirrups and slew Sir Henry with a single blow, cleaving helm and head.

Nonplussed as they were, the English nonetheless continued to advance upon the exultant Scots, but the woods concealed more of the enemy than they had at first revealed. A skirmish followed, and the English vanguard fell back towards the Torwood.

Stirling Castle, magnificently sited on its great rock, dominating the River Forth and the Carse of Stirling. The need to relieve Stirling, besieged by Edward Bruce, instigated the Banockburn campaign.

Meanwhile a force of about three hundred mounted knights, led by Sir Robert Clifford and Sir Henry de Beaumont, was carrying out a reconnaissance in force to the east of the New Park, probably exploring the possibility of outflanking the Scots and approaching Stirling across the Carse, rather than contesting the main route through the New Park. They were intercepted by a body of Scottish spearmen, led by the Earl of Moray, in a *schiltrom* – a hedge formation, aptly described as resembling a giant hedgehog bristling with spear-points. The schiltrom withstood the repeated charges of Clifford and Beaumont's knights, and after hard fighting the Scots forced them to retire.

Two repulses had brought English morale low indeed, and no further action took place that night. Edward, however, was no less determined to do battle on the morrow. The Scots had made good use of their strong position in the New Park, but the King had little doubt that they would be defeated by superior numbers if they could be enticed out of the wood to give battle on open ground. After consultation with Pembroke, Edward decided to use the night in taking his army across the Bannock Burn on to firmer ground to the east of the New Park. It was a constricted battlefield between the Bannock Burn and the Pelstream Burn, but it was firm enough for the cavalry and clear of the 'pottes', which had doubtless been discovered earlier when the vanguard advanced. The crossing of the Bannock Burn and its marshy tributaries was effected with the help of the castle garrison who came out bringing planks and doors to make bridges. Once the crossing was achieved, the English soldiery raised their morale from the ale-barrels, and the short summer night was over.

At dawn, the Scots came out of the wood. They were in four divisions, led by Edward Bruce, the Earl of Moray and Sir James Douglas, with the King in command of the rearguard. It was exactly what Edward had hoped for, that the Scottish army, composed almost entirely of infantry, would be enticed on to the open ground to be annihilated by his heavy cavalry.

Sir Ingram de Umfraville, who was at the King's side, had his doubts that the solidly massed spearmen would be annihilated so easily. He suggested to the King that if the English army withdrew beyond the tents and baggage-waggons the Scots would be tempted to break ranks by the chance of rich plunder, and could then be cut to pieces easily. The King angrily refused, saying that it was a dishonourable suggestion. It may be doubted, anyway, that King Robert's disciplined army would have acted as Umfraville supposed.

At the edge of the wood the Scottish army knelt as one man to say the Paternoster. King Edward essayed a joke: 'Yon kneeling folk for mercy pray.' Umfraville agreed, and added: 'But not from you.'

The battle began with the advance of Edward Bruce's division. The English vanguard charged them, headed by Gloucester who had had a last minute quarrel with the King.

104

Bronze figure of a
knight *c.* 1300.

Doubting the easy victory Edward prophesied, he had urged delay, Edward had accused him of cowardice, and Gloucester had flung off in a rage to prove his personal courage. In the forefront of the charge, he was one of the first to be slain.

The English vanguard fell back, and King Robert ordered Moray and Douglas to advance in support of his brother. On the constricted field, the English numbers became more of a liability than an asset. Between the two streams, they had little room to manœuvre as the Scottish spearmen pressed remorselessly in upon them. And still Robert the Bruce held his own division in reserve. One of the English commanders realised that only archers could break the Scottish schiltroms, and when the archers were brought round to shoot from the flank, the English had their one chance to redeem the battle. King Robert, however, made quick use of his light cavalry, and a sudden charge of the little force, led by Sir Robert Keith, scattered the English bowmen beyond hope of re-forming. The King of Scots then brought in his own division, and the English army was helplessly hemmed in, to be massacred between the two streams.

The victory of the Scots was already assured when the last participants in the battle arrived. King Robert had left his catering corps and camp-followers on the other side of Coxet Hill in the north of the New Park. At this point the non-combatants, perhaps having sent some enterprising individual to see how the battle was going, decided to make their own contribution to their King's victory. Having improvised some banners and armed themselves with anything which could inflict injury, they marched over the hill and out of the wood. They did not affect the outcome of the battle, but the English supposed them to be a reserve force, and so their appearance marked the English recognition of defeat.

King Edward himself, it was said, fought like a lion. He was parted from his shield-bearer, and his horse was killed under him, but he found a second horse and pressed into the thick of the fighting, determined to contest defeat to the last. The Earl of Pembroke, however, realised that if the King were killed or captured, especially the latter, King Robert could dictate what peace terms he chose. Determined, therefore, to prevent either happening, Pembroke seized the King's rein, and aided by Sir

Giles D'Argentan, dragged the unwilling Edward from the field. They gathered a force of about five hundred knights and rode for Stirling. Sir Philip Mowbray refused to admit them into the castle, pointing out that with the English defeated he was now obliged to surrender, so that to admit the King would merely be to have him captured. Edward and his knights thereupon turned about and made for Dunbar, hotly pursued by Sir James Douglas. The pro-English Earl of Dunbar gave the King shelter in his castle and then sent him by boat to Berwick, while most of the knights made their way there by land.

Pembroke, once he had seen the King on his way, returned to the field to withdraw what remained of his own contingent. With remarkable success he brought away many of his Welshmen and led them, himself walking and barefoot at the last, back home by way of Carlisle. As a feat of conscientious leadership and endurance, it is worth remembrance.

Otherwise, the fate of the English army was disastrous. The casualties, though impossible to estimate accurately, were acknowledged to be extremely heavy, and the death-roll included great numbers who were not slain in the field but drowned in the Bannock Burn and the Forth as they attempted to flee. Many more who escaped from the field were murdered

The Richard de Bury chest from the early fourteenth century. On the lid are the painted arms of the Bishop of Durham and Ralph Neville, who spent most of his life fighting the Scots.

as they endeavoured to make their way home through enemy country.

Large numbers of prisoners were also taken, including the Earl of Hereford, for whom King Robert exchanged his Queen, his sister and his daughter, captured in 1306 by Edward I. Since Hereford alone served this desired purpose, and £200,000 worth of goods in contemporary values – millions of pounds' worth in twentieth-century values – was taken from the English army and baggage-train, King Robert could afford to be generous towards the rest of his prisoners. Sir Marmaduke Tweng, who surrendered to the King personally, was permitted to return home without ransom; and Sir Ralph de Monthermer, to whom Robert the Bruce owed a debt of gratitude for once having saved him from the wrath of Edward I, was likewise freed unransomed.

King Robert showed his magnanimity in other ways: he kept a night's vigil over the body of the Earl of Gloucester, to whom he was related, and he returned the shield of King Edward which had fallen into Scottish hands when his shield-bearer, Sir Roger Northburgh, was captured. Gratitude for his victory doubtless inspired King Robert's generosity, for he had achieved more than he would have dared to hope, against great odds. 'After the aforesaid victory,' wrote the chronicler of Lanercost, 'Robert de Brus was commonly called King of Scotland by all men, because he had acquired Scotland by force of arms.'

Commenting on Edward II's defeat, the author of the *Vita Edwardi Secundi* wrote 'Indeed I think it is unheard of in our time for such an army to be scattered so suddenly by infantry, unless when the flower of France fell before the Flemings at Courtrai.' This was an extremely perceptive comment, for the battle of Courtrai, fought in 1302, was the first battle to show that well-armed, well-trained infantry, especially when pro-tected by archers, could overcome the charge of heavily-armed knights. Bannockburn likewise showed the potential superiority of well-trained infantry, though archers were used only in-effectively to support Edward's cavalry. The battle of Morgarten, at which Swiss infantry defeated the heavy cavalry of the Emperor in 1315, hammered home the same lesson, and the victories of Edward III in France later in the century further

OPPOSITE The tomb, in Westminster Abbey, of Aymer de Valence, Earl of Pembroke, the most intelligent and respected of Edward II's magnates.

endorsed it, adding the lesson that against the power of the long bow even the latest development of plate-armour was no defence.

Bannockburn, therefore, illustrated an evolution in warfare, in which Edward II was defeated because his army represented the trend which the warfare of the future would reject. He was also defeated because Robert the Bruce was the better general.

The battle of Courtrai, 1302. This was the first battle in which well-trained infantry disproved the accepted belief in the invincibility of mounted knights. The battle of Bannockburn was similarly an infantry victory.

King Edward might have acknowledged the second reason in his own mind, but he could scarcely have been aware of the first. Yet even had he been so, it would have offered him little comfort. He returned to England humiliated by defeat, his political position worse than it had been in the autumn of 1313. He returned to face Thomas of Lancaster, who had the cold effrontery to be gratified by his defeat.

111

4 The King versus

Thomas of Lancaster
1314-22

I have not yet forgotten the wrong that was done to my brother Piers.

(Words attributed to Edward II, *Vita Edwardi Secundi*)

THE EXTREMISM OF A MINORITY of the Lords Ordainers, headed by Lancaster, had in a sense redounded to the King's advantage. By the settlement of 1313 which followed Gaveston's death, Edward had gained a second chance, whereby he might have recouped his prestige if he had fought a successful campaign against Robert the Bruce. But by losing the battle of Bannockburn Edward lost that second chance, and when he returned to England in the late summer of 1314 his prestige had sunk to its lowest ebb so far.

Thomas of Lancaster had played a highly dubious part in the events of 1314. As previously mentioned, he had sent to the King at Berwick the minimum number of knights and men-at-arms permitted by his feudal obligations. But while the King was in Scotland Lancaster had raised a considerable force which he maintained in arms while he awaited the outcome of the Bannockburn campaign. He was prepared either to face Edward's hostility if he were victorious, or to impose his will upon him if he were defeated. After Bannockburn, with his army vanquished and scattered, and his supporters slain, taken prisoner or fugitive, Edward was completely at Lancaster's mercy. Lancaster therefore prepared to reap the rewards of a discreditable policy which he had pursued with some skill.

Thomas of Lancaster has been described as 'the most impossible of medieval politicians' and as 'the ideal leader for a party without ideals'. He was at his most effective in opposition, but when the King's misfortunes provided him with an opportunity to implement his own ideas, it transpired that beyond a certain enthusiasm for the Ordinances, his ideas on government were no whit superior to the King's. Even as far as the Ordinances were concerned, it is impossible to avoid the impression that Lancaster adhered to them rather as a means of increasing his power at the expense of the King's than out of any genuine enthusiasm for good government. Certainly he showed himself no more dedicated than Edward to the actual business of governing or to the routine of administration. It quickly became apparent that in politics turbulence characterised him, but intelligence did not.

When Edward left Berwick and came south to meet his Parliament at York, in September 1314, there was no concealing the weakness of his position; for with Gloucester dead, Pembroke as discredited as himself by the defeat, and Hereford a prisoner, it was impossible for him to outface the combined strength of Lancaster, Warwick, Surrey and Arundel, especially as their arguments could be supported by a show of force from Lancaster's private army which was held in readiness at Pontefract.

According to the *Vita Edwardi Secundi*,

> The earls said that the Ordinances had not been observed and therefore events had turned out badly for the King ... so that no good could come unless the Ordinances were fully observed ... . The earls said that ... if the Ordinances ought to be observed it was necessary to ask for their execution. The King granted their execution: he denied the earls nothing.

Indeed, he was in no position to do so, and during the autumn of 1314 and the spring of the following year he was obliged to endure passively the purge of the Household upon which Lancaster insisted, and the replacement of his own men by Lancastrian supporters in most of the great offices of state. Edward's friend Walter Reynolds, Archbishop of Canterbury, was replaced at the Chancery by John Sandale, and the Keeper of the Wardrobe, Ingelard Warley, who was also one of Edward's confidants, was replaced by William Melton, who shortly afterwards became Archbishop of York. He proved to be a fortunate choice, an honourable and disinterested man who gained the respect alike of the King's supporters and those of Lancaster. The King was also deprived of the company of Hugh Despenser the elder, who was obliged to retire from Court, and of Pembroke, upon whom he had chiefly relied for advice from the time of Gaveston's death to the battle of Bannockburn. Pembroke, who had never forgotten or forgiven the treachery of Lancaster and his supporters over the death of Gaveston, disassociated himself completely from the government and retired from Court while Lancaster was in power.

At this nadir of his fortunes, Edward's thoughts turned much to Gaveston; his love for his dead favourite had not faded with the passage of time. Ever since his death, Gaveston's embalmed body had remained in the care of the Oxford Dominicans, who were generously rewarded by the King for its safekeeping. Edward's intention had been to leave the body in their care until

Court Life

These scenes from Queen
Mary's Psalter illustrate some
of the entertainments of
a medieval court.

RIGHT A lady and
gentleman play chess.
BELOW A king on
a hawking party.

ABOVE Music is played
while the food is served.
RIGHT A page offers wine
to the king.

Gaveston's death had been avenged; but shortly after Christmas 1314, when it seemed that vengeance might be limitlessly deferred, Edward sought comfort for his tribulations in giving Gaveston a magnificent funeral. The church of the Dominican priory beside his favourite manor of Langley was Edward's choice for Gaveston's burial place, and the funeral rites were performed by Archbishop Reynolds, and attended by four bishops and a large concourse of clergy. Most of the magnates declined to attend, holding themselves aloof from Gaveston in death as much as in life. Their persistent animosity no doubt served to stiffen Edward's resolve that he would have his vengeance, however long he was obliged to wait for it.

Throughout 1315, Lancaster continued to consolidate his position. Besides Court and household officials, most of the sheriffs had been changed to nominees of his own, extending his network of supporters all over the country. Thanks to his enthusiasm for the Ordinances, he gained the general support of the nobility, clergy and commons, as the guardian of their privileges against the King. There was little that Edward could do but bide his time until Lancaster's selfish ambitions and incompetence should bring about the disillusionment of his supporters.

The year ended with the star of Lancaster still in the ascendant. The King more or less ignored him, and turning from his troubles to congenial amusements, he spent Christmas in Cambridgeshire, rowing in the fens 'with a great company of simple people'.

At the end of January 1316, Parliament assembled at Lincoln. Lancaster deigned to appear two weeks later, to be appointed the King's chief councillor, whose assent was required to every administrative act, and at whose behest any other member of the King's Council who was regarded as guilty of 'bad counsel' could be removed with the consent of Parliament – a Parliament which supported Lancaster. Monarchical authority, it seemed, had almost ceased to exist.

However, Lancaster soon found that his position had been attained more easily than it could be maintained, especially as he himself had an ineradicable reluctance to attend Councils and Parliaments, either because he desired to enjoy power without responsibility or because he considered it proper to

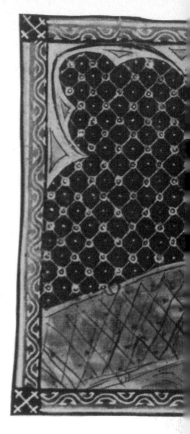

While Lancaster's party increased in strength King Edward spent his Christmas rowing in the Fens with 'simple people'.

delegate. His difficulties were increased by the fact that 1315 and
1316 were years of natural disaster throughout Europe. Flood,
famine and disease led to economic misery and political unrest.
Rebellion stirred in Wales and in England itself.

In 1315, following the death of the Earl of Gloucester at
Bannockburn, one Payne of Turberville was appointed royal
warden of Gloucester's lordship of Glamorgan. He proceeded
to displace all Gloucester's old officials, including 'a great and
powerful Welshman' named Llewellyn Bren, who retaliated by
organising a revolt. He attacked Caerphilly Castle, and caused
a great deal of slaughter and destruction, though the castle
managed to hold out against him. Nonetheless, there was some
fear that his revolt might fan a flame of rebellion throughout
Wales; and as soon as the Earl of Hereford returned from his
Scottish captivity, he was commanded to crush the rising before
it had chance to spread farther. The Marcher Lords, including
Roger Mortimer of Chirk and his nephew Roger Mortimer of

Wigmore, and Henry of Lancaster, the Lord of Kidwelly and brother of the Earl of Lancaster, all gave their support to Hereford, and the rising was quickly under control. Llewellyn Bren showed himself a man of rare courage and magnanimity, for, faced with defeat, he surrendered himself to obtain mercy for his followers. After two years' captivity, he suffered a traitor's death at Cardiff.

In the same year as Llewellyn Bren's revolt, Thomas of Lancaster faced the rebellion of Adam Banaster, one of his own Lancashire vassals. Banaster, whose chief desire was to avoid being brought to justice for a murder, attempted to win royal support by posing as the champion of the King's rights against Lancaster. Edward, however, had no time to take advantage of the situation even had he considered doing so, for the revolt was swiftly crushed by Lancaster's favourite household knight, Sir Robert Holland, who made a present to his lord of Banaster's head.

More serious trouble was caused by the revolt of Bristol, where the townsmen attempted to put an end to the rule of an oligarchy of fourteen leading citizens. A royal inquiry was held, which gave a decision in favour of the fourteen. The warden of Bristol Castle, Lord Badlesmere, gave them his support, but the burgesses of Bristol took up arms, and the judges who had conducted the inquiry fled for their lives. An attempt to bring the rioters to justice failed, and the commons of Bristol drove out the oligarchs and remained in revolt against the government until the Earl of Pembroke was prevailed upon to besiege the city. Pembroke's siege-engines overawed the Bristoleans, who surrendered, and the trouble ended with an example being made of a few ringleaders, while the mass of the citizens received a free pardon.

Though the local troubles which disturbed Wales, Lancashire and the West Country seemed serious enough, larger disturbances loomed in the background.

Ever since Bannockburn, Robert the Bruce had followed up his advantage by devastating the north of England. Sir James Douglas and the Earl of Moray led raids which penetrated as far as Furness in the west and Holderness in the east, but significantly the raiders always spared the lands of Thomas of Lancaster. When the time of reckoning came, the dubious nature of Lancaster's dealings with the Scots would greatly strengthen King Edward's case against him.

While King Robert's lieutenants raided northern England, his brother Edward Bruce invaded Ireland with the hope of winning a kingdom for himself. The background to the disturbances which troubled England and Wales was the campaign which Edward Bruce fought, successfully at first, against English rule in Ireland. His adventure lasted almost four years, beginning with his invasion in March 1315, culminating in his triumphant coronation near Dundalk, and ending with his defeat and slaughter by the English commander, Sir John de Bermingham, in October 1318. The significance of his enterprise was best summed up by T. F. Tout, who wrote that after Edward Bruce's death

> Ireland rapidly settled down into its normal condition of impotent turbulence. Though at first sight the invader utterly failed, yet he pricked the bubble of English power in Ireland. His gallant attempt at winning the throne is the critical event in a long period of Irish history. From the days of Henry III to the days of Edward Bruce, the lordship of the English Kings in Ireland was to some extent a reality. From 1315 to the reign of Henry VIII the English dominion was little more than a name as regards the greater part of Ireland.

Edward II himself had little to do with events in Ireland, apart from rewarding Sir John de Bermingham, when the business was over, with the earldom of Louth.

While the fortunes of Edward Bruce flowed and ebbed, Edward II was preoccupied by his struggle with Thomas of Lancaster. 1316 was the critical year, in which Lancaster's incompetence had begun to show itself; and Edward, who had been the passive victim of Lancaster's ascendancy throughout 1315, began to work, as he had previously worked against the Lords Ordainers, to undermine the party which opposed him.

Lancaster's attempt to enforce the Ordinances was not effective enough to prevent Edward from making some appointments of his own. Ingelard Warley, displaced from the Wardrobe, was appointed a baron of the Exchequer, and the Lancastrian Treasurer, Sir Walter Norwich, was removed in favour of John Hotham, Bishop of Ely, who had been a friend of Gaveston. Enough of Edward's household officials had

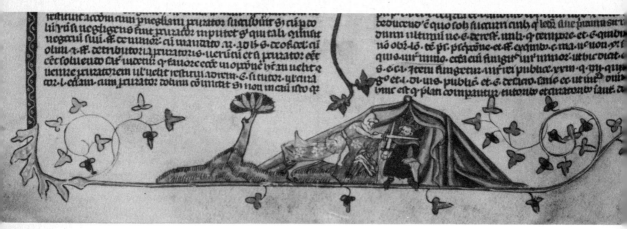

A king in his tent is attacked by a knight. Thomas of Lancaster's great resources, which enabled him to wage private war against the King, for a time reduced the royal authority to a dead letter.

survived Lancaster's original purge to give the King quite a strong party; administration became extremely difficult for Lancaster's men. The King's contemporary biographer described the uneasy situation:

> Whatever pleases the Lord King the Earl's servants try to upset; and whatever pleases the Earl the King's servants call treachery: and so, at the suggestion of the Devil, the *familiares* of each put themselves in the way and their lords, by whom the land ought to be defended, are not allowed to be of one accord.

Edward was even able to have his revenge for Lancaster's refusal to accompany him on the Bannockburn campaign. When Lancaster mounted an expedition against the Scots in 1316, Edward refused to participate, and Lancaster, who had gone as far as Newcastle, at once returned home.

Lancaster's problems were brought to a head by domestic discord. In the spring of 1317 Lancaster's wife, Alice de Lacy, daughter of the late Earl of Lincoln, ran away from him, and placing herself under the protection of the Earl of Surrey, went to live with her paramour, a mere squire named Ebulo L'Estrange. It was generally believed, and certainly believed by Lancaster, that the King had connived at her elopement. However, it was Surrey who bore the impact of Lancaster's wrath. Surrey stood by the Countess, and private war broke out between the two earls in the north.

Edward gathered an army and marched north upon the pretext of restoring order, but in reality he probably nourished

122

the hope of making common cause with Surrey and crushing Lancaster.

Lancaster, however, was still a match for him. He destroyed the bridges which lay in the path of the King's advance and 'asserted that he acted thus because he was Steward of England and it was his duty to see to the welfare of the realm and if the King wished to take up arms against anyone he ought first to warn the Steward'. This was Lancaster's first attempt to manipulate his possession of the office of Steward for his own advantage, somewhat as the Earls of Norfolk and Hereford had attempted to manipulate their offices of Earl Marshal and Constable in the previous reign. Edward did not bandy words with him. His response was to march his army beneath the walls of Pontefract in battle array, inviting Lancaster to come out and try conclusions with him. An outbreak of civil war was only prevented by the Earl of Pembroke, who had accompanied the King, and who fortunately had sufficient authority with him to act as a restraining influence. From this moment Pembroke took it upon himself to assume the role of peacemaker, and it was not long before his efforts achieved a good result.

In the meantime, with the whole country in turmoil, and the King's authority flouted everywhere, it was scarcely surprising that rumours began to circulate that the King was not the true son of his father, but a changeling. The fact that Edward closely resembled his forebears, especially his grandfather Henry III, was conveniently forgotten.

In 1318, a young man named John of Powderham took possession of the King's manor at Oxford and 'made claim to the kingdom of England, alleging that he was the true heir of the realm as the son of the illustrious King Edward who had long been dead'. In the words of the Lanercost chronicler, 'He declared that my Lord Edward, who at that time possessed the kingdom, was not of the blood royal, nor had any right to the realm, which he offered to prove by combat with him. ...' He cited the King's notorious addiction to rustic pursuits as proof that his antecedants were commensurably rustic, and adduced as further proof of his unkingly origin, his predilection for 'other vanities and frivolities wherein it doth not become a King's son to busy himself'.

John of Powderham, however, possessed no resources other

than the outrageous courage of a man in the grip of a delusion. He was easily captured and brought before the King at Northampton. Edward, who was never lacking in a certain sense of humour, greeted him ironically with the words, 'Welcome, my brother.' John of Powderham took the bull by the horns and answered: 'Thou art no brother of mine, but falsely thou claimest the kingdom for thyself. Thou hast not a drop of blood from the illustrious Edward, and that I am prepared to prove against thee or any one else in thy room.' Obviously there was nothing to be done but to place the hapless young man under arrest. He was put on trial, and admitted that he had been tempted to his imposture by an evil spirit. Accordingly he was executed by being hanged and afterwards burned.

Edward seems to have regarded the imposture as a joke; the savage end of the impostor was merely in accordance with the mood of the times. It would probably not have occurred to the King that there was anything else to be done with such a person but execute him. Queen Isabella, however, was said to have been 'troubled ... beyond measure' by the matter. Perhaps she allowed the reasoning of John of Powderham to take root in her mind. Her kindly apologist, Professor Hilda Johnstone, was inclined to feel that doubt raised in Isabella's mind might partly explain the part which she later played in her husband's downfall, since the imposture, if true, 'placed her in a position of humiliation so galling that almost any effort towards freedom, short of murder, might seem excusable'.

The imposture of John of Powderham was a nine days' wonder which died a natural death. The violence of the last few years also died down, under the pacifying influence of the Earl of Pembroke and the 'Middle Party' which he brought into being.

The Middle Party is thought to have originated at the end of 1316, when Pembroke was sent by the King on a mission to the Pope at Avignon. He was accompanied by Lord Badlesmere, the Bishop of Ely and John Salmon, Bishop of Norwich, all of whom subsequently became members of his Middle Party. Doubtless, while they were out of England they had ample opportunity to discuss the affairs of their unhappy country, and to consider a possible remedy.

OPPOSITE Fourteenth-century paintings believed to represent Henry III (left) and his grandson Edward II.

The shields of Thomas of Brotherton, Earl of Norfolk and Thomas of Woodstock, Earl of Kent, brothers to Edward II, from the Holkham version of Walter de Milemete's Treatise, *c.* 1326.

On the way back from Avignon Pembroke was seized by a French knight who claimed that the King of England owed him money for military service. Edward immediately showed his generosity and his friendship for Pembroke by paying his captor a ransom of £2,500. It is important to stress the friendly relations of Pembroke and the King, for they greatly eased the establishment of the Middle Party's ascendancy.

After his return to England, Pembroke worked hard to win more supporters, and in due course he could count upon the Earls of Surrey, Hereford and Arundel, and the King's young half-brother, Thomas of Brotherton, who had been given the title of Earl of Norfolk. (Warwick, whom Lancaster had found a difficult and indeed an unmanageable ally, had passed beyond the scope of Pembroke's persuasions; he had died in 1316.) However, Pembroke found more supporters in Hugh Despenser the elder, and the younger Despenser and his two brothers-in-law, Hugh Audley and Roger Damory. These three young men were married to the sisters of the late Earl of Gloucester, and rivalry for the largest share in the Gloucester estates soon led

126

to enmity between them, though for the time being they were prepared to work together. In addition to these barons and to the bishops who had accompanied him to Avignon, Pembroke won over Bishops Langton of Chichester and Stapledon of Exeter, and the erstwhile Lancastrian John Sandale, for whom he obtained the bishopric of Winchester.

The first objective of the Middle Party was to mediate between the King and Lancaster, to remove the threat of civil war, and then to face the problem of providing effective government.

The Middle Party was welcome to the King, despite the fact that Pembroke desired to see the Ordinances fully implemented, for Edward was willing to accept any measures which would bring about a decline of Lancaster's influence. Besides, he must have been well aware that among Pembroke's supporters were many who had joined him out of enmity for Lancaster rather than love for the Ordinances. He probably felt that co-operation with Pembroke, though it might have temporary drawbacks, could ultimately be turned to his advantage.

A series of discussions was held between Lancaster and the leaders of the Middle Party, at which it was agreed that the Ordinances should be implemented, that Lancaster and his followers should receive the customary pardons for any illegal acts they had committed (this was the usual method of taking out an insurance policy on the future), and that a standing council should be formed to advise the King, who should have no freedom to act without its advice.

Upon the basis of these discussions Lancaster and Pembroke's party negotiated the Treaty of Leake, which was signed on 9 August 1318. It was agreed that the standing council should consist of two bishops, one earl, one baron, and one knight banneret who was to be nominated by Lancaster, and that Parliament should be summoned to ratify this arrangement and to re-enact the Ordinances. Lancaster then rode south to meet and be reconciled with Edward. They met at Hathern, near Loughborough, on a bridge over the River Soar, and exchanged a kiss of peace. It was a hollow ceremony, for Lancaster refused either to be reconciled with the elder Despenser or to settle his feud with Surrey. Edward made no protestations, but a kiss of peace meant nothing while Gaveston remained unavenged.

At first sight, it seemed that Lancaster was in a strong position. He had negotiated like a prince with the Middle Party, and had retained his right to pursue his private quarrels. But in fact Lancaster had been outmanœuvred over the question of the standing council, for he himself was not to be a member of it, and his nominee was not to possess the right of veto. Lancaster was not slow to realise what had happened, and when Parliament met in October 1318 to ratify the Treaty of Leake, he attempted to recoup his position by invoking for a second time the privileges which he claimed were concomitant with his office of hereditary Steward of England.

Lancaster claimed that as Steward of England he possessed the right to nominate the Steward of the King's Household, exactly as the Earl Marshal possessed the right to nominate the Marshal of the Household. He was fobbed off with the assurance that the records would be searched to establish the validity of his claim. In the meantime, Lord Badlesmere took office as Steward of the Household, and Hugh Despenser the younger became the Chamberlain. Edward, though impatient of the limitations which were still imposed upon his sovereignty, was well satisfied to see himself surrounded by a mixture of friends and moderates, with Lancaster dislodged from the high position which he had occupied at the beginning of the year.

While the King and the magnates of England were involved in this power struggle, Berwick, the last Scottish town to remain in English hands, had fallen to Robert the Bruce. The shock of this symbolic loss had a unifying effect far more powerful than that of Pembroke's patient efforts. Over the possession of Berwick, national prestige was at stake. Pembroke, Surrey and the elder Despenser attended the muster at Newcastle in June 1319, side by side with Thomas of Lancaster and his brother Henry. Edward led an army of eight thousand men to the siege of Berwick, and Queen Isabella accompanied him as far as York.

Robert the Bruce had entrusted the defence of Berwick to his son-in-law Walter the Stewart, but he supported the Stewart brilliantly by organising an invasion of Yorkshire, led by Moray and Douglas. Queen Isabella, narrowly escaping capture, fled to the safe refuge of Nottingham, while William Melton, Archbishop of York, attempted to defend the county

OPPOSITE A king, a knight and a bishop.

and his see. The best of the Yorkshire soldiers were with the King at Berwick, but the Archbishop hastily raised a force of local farmers, York citizens, priests and monks. With Melton himself at their head, they marched out to do battle with the Scots. The Yorkshiremen encountered the seasoned campaigners of Moray and Douglas at Myton-on-Swale, not far from Boroughbridge. Inevitably, Melton's homeguard was defeated with great slaughter, and the battle came to be known as the 'Chapter of Myton' because of the large number of ecclesiastics who had taken part in it. The Archbishop himself, who had led them bravely, was fortunate enough to escape.

The Scots then advanced towards Pontefract; the siege of Berwick was abandoned, and the magnates of England scattered to defend their possessions. Significantly, Lancaster's stronghold was unharmed, and the Scots marched home by the westward route over the Pennines.

Now that Lancaster's position was no longer as strong as it had been, calumny was openly uttered. Sir Hugh Despenser the elder accused Lancaster of having attempted to betray Isabella to the Scots, and others declared that Lancaster had received huge sums of money from Robert the Bruce to 'lend him secret aid'. Lancaster denied these accusations and offered to prove his innocence by ordeal of hot iron; however, he was permitted to prove it by 'compurgation' – the sworn testimony of a number of his peers. The trouble subsided, but the King, who had been far from satisfied with Lancaster's conduct at Berwick, was said to have hinted darkly, 'When this wretched business is over we will turn our hands to other matters. For I have not yet forgotten the wrong that was done to my brother Piers.'

After the siege of Berwick had been raised Edward and Pembroke negotiated a two years' truce with King Robert. The failure before Berwick and the ensuing truce were severe blows to the prestige of the Middle Party, and Lancaster showed his awareness of this fact by declining to attend the Parliament which met at York in January 1320. But Lancaster's own position had been damaged by rumours of his dubious relations with the Scots. The way was open for Edward to derive what advantage he could from a situation which offered him his first chance since 1313 to recoup his authority.

When Edward went to France in the early summer of 1320 to pay homage to the new French King, Philip V, for Aquitaine and Ponthieu, he appointed Pembroke as his Regent and Lord Badlesmere as Warden of the Cinque Ports. But after his return it gradually became apparent that the two leaders of the Middle Party were less and less in the King's confidence, and that their place at the centre of affairs was being taken by the two Despensers.

Sir Hugh Despenser the elder, who had been a trusted servant of Edward I, was about sixty years of age, and he had been throughout the reign the most unswerving of Edward II's adherents. He had stood by the King throughout the Gaveston troubles, even when his own son had joined the Lord Ordainers, and though driven from Court by the enmity of Lancaster and his adherents more than once, he had never remained long away from the King, and had never indulged in the slightest political flirtation with his enemies. He had supported the Middle Party as representing the King's best interests. He possessed administrative ability and political acumen, and he was described by Bishop Stubbs as an 'honourable, prudent, industrious and energetic old man'. He had one vice, however, which especially did not commend him to his contemporaries: intense acquisitiveness, and the rewards which he expected for his services to the King had naturally to be provided at the expense of his political enemies.

His son was an even more unpopular figure. Hugh Despenser the younger was the exact contemporary of the King, and had been knighted on the day that Edward became Prince of Wales. He was described by Stubbs, with adjectives derived from various contemporary chronicles, as 'ambitious, cruel, haughty and abandoned'; but Edward liked him and perhaps more than liked him. According to the Lanercost chronicler, he became 'as it were, the King of England's right eye and, after the death of Piers de Gaveston, his chief counsellor against the earls and barons'. Of course, this statement does not convey the fact that the development of Hugh Despenser's intimacy with the King had been very gradual. Though he had been a member of Edward's household when he was Prince of Wales, as one of the committee which drew up the Ordinances he had been among Edward's opponents. After Gaveston's death, he had once more

'An honourable, prudent, industrious and energetic old man'

131

returned to the King's party, and had begun to enjoy his favour about the time of the Bannockburn campaign. Thereafter he had become increasingly close to the King, who had shown him great favour by marrying him to Eleanor de Clare, the eldest of the three sisters of the Earl of Gloucester.

Hugh Despenser the younger had all his father's ability, but he far surpassed him in acquisitiveness and ambition. His marriage to Eleanor de Clare gave him aspirations to the earldom of Gloucester also, but the pursuit of this ambition was complicated by the fact that Gloucester's sisters had been his co-heiresses, and the husbands of the other two sisters could lay claim to the earldom with as much or as little right as Hugh Despenser. In 1317 the Gloucester estates had been divided with reasonable fairness between the husbands of the three sisters. Hugh Despenser had received the lordship of Glamorgan; Hugh Audley, who had married the second sister, Margaret de Clare, Gaveston's widow, had received Newport and Netherwent; and Roger Damory, who had married the youngest sister, Elizabeth, received the castle and lordship of Usk.

Hugh Despenser, once he had established his ascendancy in the political scene and in the King's favour, embarked upon a policy of territorial aggrandisement in Wales, partly at the expense of his two brothers-in-law, whereby he hoped to acquire a vast and centralised bloc of estates to which the Gloucester title might be added in the course of time. Despenser's aggression had the effect of reviving old enmities, for Damory looked to Pembroke to protect his interests, while Audley sought the protection of Lancaster. However, Despenser was initially successful. First he induced Audley to exchange Newport for estates in England; next he obtained from the King a grant of Dryssllwyn Castle and Cantrefmawr to the west of Glamorgan and of the Isle of Lundy which lies between South Wales and the coast of North Devon, a useful base from which to command the Bristol Channel.

These acquisitions were sufficient to arouse the enmity of the Marcher Lords, but it was Despenser's dealings with the lands of Sir William de Braose, Lord of Gower, which finally united them against him. Sir William de Braose, the last male heir of a great family which had fallen into poverty, had hoped to find a purchaser for his estates among the Marcher Lords. However,

OPPOSITE Fourteenth-century armorial bearings on enamel plaques which were originally worn on a belt.

133

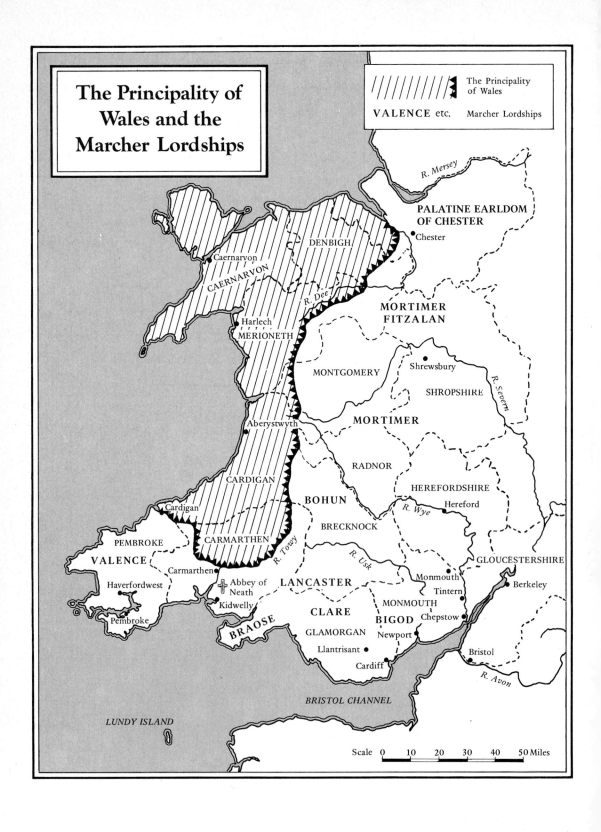

The Principality of Wales and the Marcher Lordships

The Principality of Wales

VALENCE etc.   Marcher Lordships

PALATINE EARLDOM OF CHESTER
Chester

R. Mersey

DENBIGH

Caernarvon

CAERNARVON

R. Dee

MORTIMER FITZALAN

Harlech
MERIONETH

MONTGOMERY

Shrewsbury

SHROPSHIRE

R. Severn

MORTIMER

Aberystwyth

RADNOR

HEREFORDSHIRE

CARDIGAN

BOHUN

Hereford

R. Wye

Cardigan

BRECKNOCK

CARMARTHEN

R. Towy

PEMBROKE

VALENCE

Carmarthen

R. Usk

GLOUCESTERSHIRE

Monmouth

Haverfordwest

Abbey of Neath

LANCASTER

Tintern

Berkeley

Kidwelly

MONMOUTH

Pembroke

CLARE

BIGOD

Chepstow

BRAOSE

GLAMORGAN

Newport

Llantrisant

Cardiff

Bristol

R. Avon

BRISTOL CHANNEL

LUNDY ISLAND

Scale   0   10   20   30   40   50 Miles

he died in the midst of his negotiations, and his son-in-law, Sir John Mowbray, in accordance with the accepted 'Customs of the March' at once seized his lands of Gower and Swansea in right of his wife. Despenser, seeing a good opportunity for further acquisition, suggested to the King that under English law Mowbray should have had a royal licence to take possession of the Braose lands, and that since he had acted without one, it could be argued that they had escheated to the Crown. The King agreed, to the horror of the Marcher Lords who immediately saw the danger to themselves inherent in the situation if English law were admitted superior to their own cherished 'Custom of the March'.

Hereford, Damory, Audley, Mowbray, the two Lords Mortimer, and Lancaster, who was an interested party because his brother was Lord of Kidwelly, all allied against Despenser, with the avowed intention of driving him and his father into exile.

Civil war threatened, and Pembroke admitted the failure of the Middle Party by giving his support to the King, who raised his forces, marched as far as Gloucester, and thence issued a command to the Marcher Lords to keep the peace. Hereford replied for the Marchers that if peace were to be maintained Parliament must be summoned to settle the problem, and that in the interim period Hugh Despenser should be placed in the custody of Lancaster. Despenser expressed perfect willingness to appear before Parliament, but naturally refused to submit himself to Lancaster's custody, whereupon the Marchers, fearing that they might not get what they wanted through the orderly channels of debate, showed their enmity to Despenser by ravaging Glamorgan.

By this time, May 1321, the King had retired from Gloucester and had summoned Parliament for July. It was obvious that the session would be a stormy one, for hatred of the Despensers had brought a vigorous opposition into being once again, of which Lancaster assumed the leadership.

Lancaster used the late spring and early summer attempting to unite as many disaffected magnates, barons and lesser men as possible into an organised opposition party pledged to secure the downfall of the Despensers. To this end he summoned two assemblies, which themselves somewhat resembled miniature

Westminster Abbey and the City of London. It was at Westminster that Edward was finally forced to agree to the banishment of the Despensers.

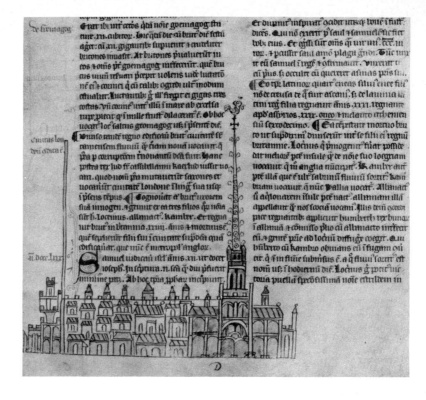

Parliaments, the first at Pontefract at the end of May, and the second at Sherburn-in-Elmet, near York, at the end of June. The first was an assembly principally of northern barons, the second was attended by some southerners and a preponderance of Marchers. To the second assembly Lancaster also invited Archbishop Melton and the Bishops of Durham and Carlisle, who came attended by a great number of lesser clergy. Melton, who favoured neither party, may have attended with the hope of being able to exert a moderating influence on Lancaster. The clergy and barons debated apart, the clergy concluding that grievances should be settled in a regular manner when Parliament met the following month. The deliberations of the laymen were not recorded, but documents survive to show that they pledged themselves formally to attempt the destruction of the Despensers.

Lancaster did not secure the overwhelming support which he had hoped for, since the greatest of the northern families held themselves aloof from him, still suspecting him of treasonable relations with the Scots. But he achieved enough support to feel fairly satisfied of his power to bring about the downfall of his enemies.

In July, Parliament sat at Westminster. It appears that Lancaster's attack on the Despensers was prefaced by the most elaborate claims which had so far been made for the privileges properly belonging to the office of Steward of England. Lancaster's adherents were probably less than enthusiastic supporters of his claim that the Steward should be responsible for every detail of the administration and permitted to dismiss negligent officials and evil councillors; but they backed him vigorously enough when he opened his attack on the Despensers. Furthermore, the Marcher Lords who had lately ravaged Glamorgan prepared to intimidate the King by bringing to London strong armed followings. Hereford, Audley, Damory and the Mortimers occupied the city, cutting off the King in Westminster Palace from his military supplies in the Tower of London.

At first, Edward attempted to resist the demands made by Lancaster and his confederates, but their reply was that unless he submitted 'they would utterly renounce their homage and set up another ruler'. It was Pembroke who persuaded him to submit, and the author of the *Vita Edwardi Secundi* reported the words which he is said to have used: 'Consider, Lord King, the power of the barons; take heed of the danger that threatens; neither brother nor sister should be dearer to thee than thyself. Do not therefore for any living soul lose thy kingdom. "He perishes on the rocks that loves another more than himself." ... '

These words imply that the King's attachment to Hugh Despenser the younger was very strong; nonetheless Edward was overawed by the magnates' threat to renounce their homage. No doubt the fact that Pembroke lent his support to the demands of the opposition also sufficiently impressed him. Isabella too is said to have urged him to submit; the rise of Hugh Despenser had certainly been no source of pleasure to her.

On 19 August judgment was given in Parliament against both the Despensers, who were sentenced to banishment and forfeiture. The session ended with the usual pardons being issued to Lancaster and his supporters.

Hugh Despenser the elder submitted to his sentence, and at once prepared to leave England. Edward showed the direction

of his sympathies by escorting him to Harwich, whence he
sailed. Despenser the younger did not leave immediately. At
first he was given refuge by the sailors of the Cinque Ports, and
then, with their assistance he 'became a sea-monster' – that is,
he took to piracy, a career which he pursued for a short time
with considerable success.

The events of 1321 are strongly reminiscent of those of 1311.
Like Gaveston, though for different reasons, Hugh Despenser
the younger had provoked against himself a coalition of
magnates sufficiently strong to drive him and his father into
exile. And as in 1311, though Edward was forced to submit to
the banishment and forfeiture of his favourite, he was determined to reverse the situation at the earliest opportunity.

That opportunity came more swiftly than Edward at his most
sanguine could have envisaged. It was facilitated by the fact
that the opposition had concerted no programme beyond
achieving the exile of the Despensers, and showed no cohesion
once the immediate success had been attained.

The occasion of Edward's completely unforeseen triumph
was an apparently minor incident which occurred in the
autumn.

On the evening of 13 October 1321 Queen Isabella, who was
going on pilgrimage to Canterbury, requested a night's lodging
at the royal castle of Leeds, near Maidstone, of which Lord
Badlesmere was the governor. At this time, Badlesmere was in
an unfortunate position, because he was extremely unpopular
with the King as one who had supported Lancaster against the
Despensers; and he was equally unpopular with Lancaster
because he still held office as Steward of the Household against
Lancaster's wishes.

When Isabella arrived at Leeds Castle Badlesmere was not in
residence, but Lady Badlesmere was there, and when she heard
of the Queen's arrival, knowing of her husband's unpopularity
at Court she lost her head completely and refused the Queen
admittance. Isabella was naturally furious. She betook herself
to a nearby priory, and ordered her entourage to force an
entrance to the castle. The Badlesmere retainers resisted, and six
of Isabella's men were killed. Incensed at the insult offered to
herself and to the Crown, Isabella complained to Edward, who
resolved to visit the Badlesmeres with heavy punishment.

138

The righteous anger of the King won him remarkably strong support. He summoned the levies of the south-eastern counties, enlisted mercenary soldiers, and called upon the magnates to support him. To the siege of Leeds Castle came Pembroke, Arundel, Richmond and Surrey, and the King's half-brothers, Thomas of Brotherton, Earl of Norfolk and Edmund of Woodstock, Earl of Kent. On 31 October, after a siege of one week, the castle fell. Thirteen of the garrison were hanged, and Lady Badlesmere was imprisoned in Dover Castle.

In the meantime Lord Badlesmere had sought what support he could for an essentially bad cause. Only Hereford and the two Mortimers had responded. They brought their forces as far as Kingston-on-Thames, and there received the news that Leeds Castle had fallen to the King.

Suddenly, and indeed fortuitously, Edward found himself in the strong position *vis-à-vis* his enemies which he had hitherto sought in vain. He had a strong army, strengthened with the confidence which comes from gaining a success. Some of the Marcher Lords were in arms, and since they had moved in support of Badlesmere they had committed an act of rebellion; Edward had an excuse to attack them, and as they were not all united against him, an excellent prospect of victory. They headed for home after the fall of Leeds, and the King set off in pursuit of them.

Lancaster, who had kept a close watch on events but made no move, began to muster his forces in November. He was completely unconcerned with the fate of Lord Badlesmere, but he realised that if Edward were successful against the Marcher Lords, then he himself would most likely be the next target for the King's enmity. By making military preparations Lancaster invited this very result.

At Doncaster, he held another assembly of his adherents, and thence issued a document which has come to be called the 'Doncaster Petition', in which the King was accused of maintaining the younger Despenser in his career of piracy, and threatened with rebellion if he did not redress this and other grievances. Edward's answer was to cause the Convocation of Canterbury, at the direction of Archbishop Reynolds, to declare invalid the sentence pronounced by Parliament against the two Despensers. By mid-January they were back in England.

The King had taken up his headquarters at Cirencester, where he kept his Christmas Court. In the new year he opened his campaign, advancing up the Severn Valley on the east bank of the river, in pursuit of Hereford, the Mortimers, Damory, Audley and Mowbray, who retreated up the west bank, holding the bridges against him. Edward was well supported by one of

140

his household knights, Sir Gruffyd Lloyd, who raised a Welsh force to harass the enemy in the rear.

Edward took his army across the Severn at Shrewsbury, where the Mortimers and Audley surrendered without a fight. Hereford, Damory and Mowbray fled north to join Lancaster, who was now at Pontefract. The King sent the Mortimers as prisoners to the Tower, and Audley to the castle of Wallingford. He then turned southward through the Marches, taking possession of the strongholds of his enemies. The last castle which fell to him was Berkeley, near Bristol, which he entered in triumph, unaware that a few years hence it would be the setting for the last scene of his life.

His bloodlessly victorious campaign in the Marches further increased the strength of Edward's position. At the beginning of 1322, he was ready for the great conflict of the reign. It was a conflict which he had long desired, for it provided him at last with his opportunity to avenge the death of Gaveston, and to destroy the rival who had been a thorn in his flesh throughout his reign. In its larger significance, in the words of a historian of the present century, it would be 'a conflict of principle between monarchy under control, and a monarchy free and unfettered'.

There is some evidence that Lancaster prepared for the conflict by reaching a secret agreement with Robert the Bruce. Certainly there was every appearance of an understanding between Lancaster and the Scots, for King Robert's raids continued to devastate Northumberland, Durham and the north of Yorkshire, but Lancaster, with his private army mustered at Pontefract, did not retaliate.

When Edward moved up to Coventry and there gathered his forces in readiness to march north, Lancaster besieged the royal castle of Tickhill, just south of Doncaster. The siege was both pointless and unsuccessful, and after three wasted weeks, Lancaster advanced south to Burton-on-Trent. However, he was out-manœuvred by Edward who evaded him and managed to cross the Trent north of Lancaster's position. Lancaster, therefore, hastily retreated north again, anxious to prevent Edward's cutting him off from his headquarters at Pontefract.

Edward, in the meantime, had been visited by Sir Andrew Harclay, the Warden of Carlisle, who had mustered the levies of Cumberland and Westmorland against the Scots. He had

uant li rois vit les gieus molt li vint a plesir

Comment ..... fint moustre a ron

Two knights in combat
from *The Romance of
Alexander* 1334–44
(Bodleian MS 264 F109).

come to impress upon Edward the grave danger to the north
of England from continuous Scottish incursions, and to urge
him to take action; but Edward ordered him to treat the
Scottish menace as of secondary importance, and to bring his
troops into action against Lancaster.

The King then advanced towards Pontefract, capturing on
his way Lancaster's castle of Tutbury, in which he took prisoner
Roger Damory, who was mortally wounded and died three
days later.

Lancaster, with Hereford, Clifford and Mowbray, retired
northwards beyond Pontefract, possibly with the expectation

142

of finding reinforcements from Scotland. Instead, they found Harclay's force defending the bridge which crossed the river Ure at Boroughbridge, north of York.

Harclay was a good general, upon whom the lessons of Courtrai, Bannockburn and Morgarten had not been wasted. His army awaited Lancaster in schiltrom formation, supported on both flanks by bodies of archers.

Lancaster divided his forces. Hereford and Clifford, in command of the infantry, attempted to take the bridge by direct assault, while Lancaster himself sought to take his cavalry across the river by a nearby ford, to attack the enemy in the flank. The attack on the bridge was unsuccessful, for Hereford, bravely leading, was himself first upon the bridge where he was killed by an upward spear-thrust from between the planking. Clifford was wounded and taken prisoner, and the infantry fell back, discomfited by the loss of both commanders. Lancaster was no more successful at the ford, for Harclay's archers inflicted heavy losses on his cavalry, and when he saw the failure of the attack on the bridge he retreated and sent to Harclay requesting a truce until the following day.

That day, 17 March 1322, saw Lancaster's final defeat, for most of Hereford's men had deserted before morning, while reinforcements from York had arrived to join Harclay. Accepting that the situation was beyond recovery, Lancaster surrendered. The credit for the victory belongs to Sir Andrew Harclay, but the credit for the successful campaign must be given to Edward himself.

While Lancaster had marched north to meet defeat, Edward had occupied Pontefract and established himself in Lancaster's great stronghold, to which Lancaster was now brought back a prisoner. In the great hall of his castle, he faced the King and his peers, men who, with the shifting configurations of political alliance had sometimes been his friends, sometimes his enemies. There was no doubt now, whatever the personal feelings of some of them may have been, that they had assembled to sentence Lancaster to death as a traitor. His recent actions, which the King himself set on record for the consideration of everyone present, could not admit of any other interpretation but that of treason.

The King was resolved to avenge the death of Gaveston, but

A pilgrim badge showing six scenes from the life and martyrdom of the unofficially canonised 'St Thomas of Lancaster'.

he was satisfied that Lancaster should suffer no more than he had inflicted. Accordingly, having sentenced Lancaster to a traitor's death, Edward commuted the sentence to that of beheading.

Lancaster met his end on 22 March. Garbed as a penitent and mounted on 'a lean white jade without bridle', he was led from his castle to a small hill outside the walls. The townspeople, who had lately shown him respect as their lord, crowded around to jeer and pelt him with snow. It might have given him either comfort or bitter amusement, could he have known that within a few months they would be venerating him as a martyr. His execution was swiftly accomplished, and, with the King's permission, his body was buried before the high altar of Pontefract priory. Clifford and Mowbray were later hanged in York, and Badlesmere in Canterbury.

The victory of Boroughbridge and the execution of Lancaster marked the high point of Edward's reign, for they represented not only the achievement of his long-deferred vengeance, but also the victory of his determination to recover the unfettered sovereignty which Lancaster would have denied him. Christopher Marlowe, in his play *Edward II*, summed up the result of Boroughbridge with accuracy and economy:

> 'Edward this day hath crown'd him
> King anew.'

5
The She-Wolf
of France
1322-6

I shall become a she-wolf
Ranging bare-toothed through the scrub
Not resting
Until earth covers Edward ...
Ranging like a she-wolf ...
Drenched by the rain of exile
Hardened by foreign winds ...

(Bertolt Brecht,
The Life of Edward II of England,
translated by Jean Benedetti)

EDWARD II, when first he became King, had enjoyed the goodwill of his magnates, and had speedily forfeited it through the follies into which he had been led by his love for Gaveston. He had been fortunate in that the settlement of 1313, following Gaveston's death, had given him a chance to redeem his reputation. But he had failed disastrously to exploit that second chance, and his defeat at Bannockburn had initiated his long struggle with Thomas of Lancaster. His victory, so unforeseeable until the last moment, provided him, almost miraculously as it must have seemed, with a third chance to assert himself and to rule his country with the unfettered authority which he conceived it right for a King to possess.

After his victory Edward summoned Parliament to meet at York, where it assembled on 22 May 1322, ready to enact all that the King desired: the punishment of the lesser rebels, the reward of deserving supporters, the repeal of the Ordinances. An innovation of the York Parliament was that it included twenty-four representatives for Wales.

It was after this Parliament that Badlesmere, Clifford and Mowbray met their ends, and fifteen other barons and knights also suffered a traitor's death. The Mortimers and Audley, who remained imprisoned, were fortunate to escape execution; no doubt Edward showed mercy in consideration of their surrender. In the case of Mortimer of Wigmore it was a mercy which he subsequently had cause to regret.

Edward's generosity to his friends must have seemed in contemporary eyes to have exceeded his severity to his enemies. Sir Andrew Harclay was rewarded with the earldom of Carlisle, and Sir Hugh Despenser the elder with the earldom of Winchester. Surprisingly the younger Despenser did not receive the Gloucester title to which he had aspired. There are various possible explanations for this unexpected self-restraint on Edward's part, for there is no doubt of his desire to advance and reward his favourite as generously as was in his power. Possibly he had learned a lesson from the past, and, remembering the violent revulsion of feeling among the magnates aroused by Gaveston's elevation to the earldom of Cornwall, had decided against bestowing upon Despenser the title which had previously belonged to his royal nephew. Or possibly, in creating the elder Despenser, an old man by the standards of the

148

The female dress of the
time is illustrated by
this brass rubbing of Dame
Jone de Kobeham, 1320.

time, Earl of Winchester, his intention was that the younger Despenser should acquire an earldom more discreetly, by inheriting it from his father in the course of some few years. However, the younger Despenser received territorial rewards on a vast scale. From Lancaster's widow he received the manors of Donnington and Bisham, and from Damory's widow the lordship of Usk. From the forfeited lands of Mowbray he was granted the castles of Swansea, Oystermouth, Pennard and Loughor, and from those of Mortimer of Chirk, the castles of Blaen Llyfni and Bwlch y Dinas, and the lordship of Talgarth. The Earl of Norfolk was obliged to give him a life-grant of the castle and honour of Chepstow and of the Welsh lands which had belonged to the old Bigod earls of Norfolk. Despenser the younger, though he received no earldom, had indeed little cause for complaint.

The Countess of Lancaster, who lost besides many castles and manors some one hundred and seventy-five knights' fees which were granted to the two Despensers, was enabled by Lancaster's death to claim the reward which she most desired: she married Ebulo L'Estrange, with whom she had lived since 1317.

Important as was the question of punishment and rewards, the chief work of the York Parliament was the repeal of the Ordinances. Much learned controversy has taken place concerning the statute of repeal, which concluded with the words:

> ... things which are to be established for the estate of the King and his heirs, and for the estate of the realm and people, shall be treated, granted and established in Parliament by our lord the King and with the consent of the prelates, earls and barons and of *the commonalty of the realm*, as has been hitherto accustomed.

The italicised words have been the cause of the controversy, since some historians have held them to mean 'the commons in Parliament', while others have pointed out that they will not bear this interpretation since they are followed by the words 'as has been hitherto accustomed', whereas the presence of the commons had not hitherto been regarded as the essential concomitant of legislative procedure.

Professor May McKisack's very sensible comment is,

> ... in the text, the inclusion of the commons, if they are included, appears to be almost incidental; the words 'commonalty of the

realm' read like the kind of phrase which runs readily off the pen of a well-trained clerk, and it is possible that the intention is merely to reinforce the notion of universal consent dear to mediaeval political theorists.

It is possible, also, that the legislators of 1322, concerned as they were to rectify the errors of the past rather than to define the constitution of the future, wished to stress that the Ordinances had been the work of a baronial oligarchy not of the King in Parliament; and therefore their concern with the future was merely the prevention of further legislation by oligarchy. The right of the commons to be consulted upon legislation arose almost incidentally.

At the time, the most obvious effect of the repeal of the Ordinances was to restore the King to the full regality which he had not possessed since before 1311. The most remarkable aspect of Edward's recovery of power was the moderation with which he used it, which argues some intelligence on his part. The political sense of the younger Despenser must be seen in the reforms of 1322; but Edward deserves a little credit for being amenable to his favourite's ideas.

Some of the Ordinances, those which aimed at administrative improvement and at safeguarding individual liberties, those which sought to regulate purveyance, to limit the powers of royal officials (significantly that of the Steward), and those which attempted to curb outlawry, were re-enacted under the name of 'Establishments'. A distinguished modern scholar made the pertinent comment that 'few seemed to realise the magnanimity of the King in adopting the good reforms of his bitterest enemies'.

Shortly after Parliament concluded its session at York, the two-year truce with Scotland, which had been signed after the unsuccessful siege of Berwick, expired. Robert the Bruce took the initiative, and in July he himself led a raid which penetrated into England as far as Preston.

Edward retaliated by ordering a muster at Newcastle, whence he advanced into southern Scotland in August. Berwick was attacked, but held out as successfully as before. Edward continued to advance, but King Robert relied upon the well-tried policy of scorched earth, and, according to John Barbour,

Examples of the fine art in the fourteenth-
century churches.
BELOW A misericorde from Wells Cathedral.
BOTTOM Scroffito tiles from Tring Church
showing scenes from the miracles of Christ.
OPPOSITE Angel from the Doom window in
Wells Cathedral.

the English army found no better supplies or booty than one lame cow in all Lothian. The best, or worst, that Edward could do was to sack the Abbey of Holyrood before retiring into England.

Before he recrossed the Border, however, he was attacked near Melrose by a force under Sir James Douglas, which inflicted some damage and withdrew unharmed. Shortly afterwards, Robert the Bruce re-entered England, from the west as before, and advanced into Yorkshire. Edward, thinking that hostilities were now over, was lodged unsuspectingly at Rievaulx Abbey with Queen Isabella. The Earl of Richmond, who was in command of part of the English army, met King Robert with Douglas and Moray near Old Byland, and was defeated and captured. Edward escaped from the Yorkshire coast by way of Bridlington, while Isabella fled north-east and took ship at Tynemouth, only just escaping capture for the second time in little more than two years.

The significance of this defeat can be seen in its effect upon the morale of northern England. Since 1311, the northern counties had suffered systematic devastation at the hands of the Scots. While Edward was involved in his struggle with Thomas of Lancaster, his northern subjects could at least hope that once his troubles were over he would give his attention to the problems of their defence. But when the victory of Borough-bridge at last gave him that opportunity, he was immediately out-generalled by Robert the Bruce, and then northern England showed that it had despaired of him.

The monks of Bridlington, with whom the King had sought refuge in his flight, obtained from Archbishop Melton per-mission to treat with the excommunicated enemy for their future immunity from attack. Accordingly they entered negotiations with the Scots, but at the same time shipped their treasure across the Humber to the relative safety of Lincolnshire. The Archbishop of York, mindful above all of the well-being of his flock, gave permission to the heads of many other religious houses to make similar arrangements.

A much more alarming reaction, however, was that of Sir Andrew Harclay, the new Earl of Carlisle, who had himself been present at the defeat of Old Byland. After his return to Carlisle, he disbanded his troops, and followed King Robert to

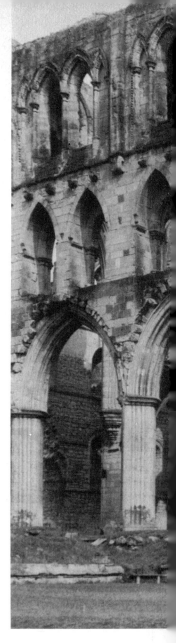

Rievaulx Abbey, where Edward and Isabella were staying when Robert the Bruce advanced into Yorkshire.

the castle of Lochmaben, near Dumfries. There he presented to the Scottish King a scheme for a final peace between Scotland and England. Robert the Bruce should receive official recognition as King of Scots in return for a cash payment in consideration of which King Edward should renounce his claim to be overlord of Scotland. Other peace terms should be settled by a commission of six Scottish lords and six English lords, and the peace should be cemented in customary fashion by an Anglo-Scottish royal marriage.

The intention of the Earl of Carlisle may have been to present to King Edward the groundwork for a solution of the Scottish problem. This is the most charitable hypothesis which can be offered for his actions. However, unhappily for him, his diplomacy was discovered in its early stages, and inevitably the worst construction was put upon it. Furthermore, he had extracted from King Robert an agreement that if the Scots should invade England in future, his own estates should be unharmed. As Edward's most recent biographer has justly remarked, 'bargaining for private immunity is not the concomitant of honest diplomacy', and by this agreement. if not by his unwarranted intervention in high politics, Carlisle branded himself a traitor.

Upon the discovery of his doings, he was arrested in his own castle of Carlisle, tried and sentenced to death. He was executed with the customary severities on 3 March 1323. However, his appreciation of the fact that Robert the Bruce had won the Scottish War of Independence was intelligent enough, and his death was followed by the opening of official peace negotiations between the King of England and the King of Scots.

It was upon the question of King Robert's right to that very title that the negotiations broke down. Edward II had inherited from his father the English claim to overlordship of Scotland, and from his own viewpoint it would have been a betrayal of his inheritance to relinquish that claim. Personal obstinacy and considerations of national prestige contributed to his determination not to accede to King Robert's demand. However, King Robert was in a strong enough position to refuse to sign a peace treaty on any other terms. In the end, the Earl of Pembroke and the younger Despenser negotiated a thirteen-year truce, which was signed at Bishopthorpe, near York, on 30 May.

The prospect of a long period without the interruption of recurrent warfare in the north provided Edward and his chosen advisers with an excellent opportunity to establish the recovered monarchical authority yet more firmly, and to tackle administrative and financial problems far more authoritatively than had been possible for any of the successive factions of recent years.

Hugh Despenser and his father, Winchester, were fortunate

in that for the time being they had no political rivals to contest their ascendancy. In the years between Bannockburn and Boroughbridge, England had teemed with ambitious magnates, but it did so no longer. Lancaster, Warwick and Hereford were dead; Badlesmere and Damory were dead. The Mortimers and Audley were still imprisoned. Richmond, who had never been a very active politician, was a prisoner in Scotland. Arundel and Surrey had always been followers rather than leaders in any political grouping. The same could be said of the King's half-brothers, Norfolk and Kent; these two young men, now in their early twenties, showed few signs of political aptitude. Lancaster's brother Henry, who had been permitted to succeed to the earldom of Leicester, was a mild-tempered man who had inherited none of his brother's ambitions. Pembroke, after years spent endeavouring to act as a moderating influence upon the violence and vagaries of his contemporaries, was clearly tiring. Possibly he was thankful to discover that Edward's new favourite was at least a man of political ability; at all events, during the last years of his life he gave his support to the régime of Hugh Despenser.

As the Lanercost chronicler observed, Hugh Despenser became 'as it were, the King of England's right eye', and from the time of Boroughbridge onwards, it was obvious that he was as firmly established in the King's affections as ever Gaveston had been. He was, however, a favourite of a very different kind. While Gaveston had been the very personification of youthful folly, Despenser was able and mature. Perhaps partly for this reason, partly because the chroniclers in castigating Despenser confined themselves largely to charges of arrogance and avarice, those historians who have accepted that Edward's relationship with Gaveston was homosexual have been inclined to assume that his relationship with Despenser was not. But there are some indications that the second relationship was of the same nature as the first, even if it was more discreetly conducted. For instance, Pembroke's strongly-worded warning to Edward in 1321, 'he perishes on the rocks that loves another more than himself', certainly implies that the King's feelings towards Despenser were evidently stronger than those of friendship. Then, after 1322, there is the evidence of Queen Isabella's hatred of Despenser, which was of such virulent intensity that it must

'He perishes on the rocks that loves another more than himself'

be regarded as one of the major causes of Edward's downfall.

The marriage of the King and Queen had begun unhappily, when Edward was in love with Gaveston; but after Gaveston's death they seem to have decided, like many other couples, to co-exist in a state of marital truce. Between 1312 and 1321 their marriage, if not happy, was at least not wholly unsuccessful. Isabella bore her husband four children: Edward, born in the year of Gaveston's death; John of Eltham, born in 1316; Eleanor of Woodstock, born in 1318; and Joan of the Tower, born in 1321. In that year Isabella had added her persuasions to those of Pembroke in urging Edward to agree to the exile of both Despensers. In 1322, the year in which the younger Despenser was finally established as Edward's favourite and the most powerful man in England, an estrangement between Edward and his Queen was first rumoured. The favour which Edward showed Despenser was undoubtedly the cause, for enmity between the Queen and the favourite soon showed itself. Besides resenting Despenser's power, it seems probable that Isabella, remembering Gaveston, may have concluded that Despenser likewise was her husband's lover. The belief that she was once again the victim of the most insulting form of infidelity would sufficiently explain Isabella's future actions, which were to win for her the grim name of the 'She-Wolf of France'.

When Isabella showed her hostility, Despenser, like Gaveston before him, treated her with contempt. But Isabella was no longer the young Queen who had helplessly endured the sight of her husband's favourite adorned with her own jewels, and had been abandoned with the royal luggage at Newcastle. She had grown into a formidable woman who was not prepared to endure unavenged humiliations. She resolved upon the destruction of both Hugh Despenser and his father, and, seemingly living down her resentment, she dissembled her hatred until her opportunity should arise.

In the meantime Hugh Despenser set about the work which won him the admiration of many later historians: the solution of Edward's administrative and financial problems. In this tremendous task he had the assistance of several men of high ability. Walter Stapledon, Bishop of Exeter, who had had the experience of a previous period in that office, was Treasurer from 1322 to 1325. He was followed by the equally able Archbishop of York, who held office from 1325 to 1326. Robert Baldock, Archdeacon of Middlesex and Keeper of the Privy Seal, who has been described as an administrator of brilliance, became Chancellor in 1323. Despenser himself, who had originally been appointed Chamberlain in 1318, held office apart from his brief period of exile until the end of the reign.

Under the aegis of Despenser, Stapledon concentrated upon reducing the chaotic Exchequer records to some sort of order, introducing a new and more efficient system of classification. According to Professor Tout, it is largely thanks to Stapledon 'that our vast collection of exchequer records before 1323 is still preserved to us'. He also enlarged the Exchequer staff, and initiated new methods of accounting, which considerably simplified the work of his successors.

When Robert Baldock became Chancellor he retained the Keepership of the Privy Seal and Controllership of the Wardrobe. During his period as Chancellor, both these offices, which had hitherto enjoyed the status of semi-autonomous departments of state, became more or less amalgamated into a non-departmentalised secretariat under the authority of the Chancery. This arrangement was, however, short-lived, and after the fall of Edward II the department of the Privy Seal developed, in Tout's words, into 'a small, independent chancery', while the Wardrobe, which Baldock's reforms had robbed of some of its former responsibilities, declined in importance throughout the rest of the century.

Despenser himself concentrated upon increasing the importance of the Chamber as a department of state. The purpose of this development was not so much to enhance the importance of his own office of Chamberlain as to enable the King to 'live of his own' independently of the Exchequer. This showed an intelligent appreciation of the lessons of the past, for had the King possessed a sufficient degree of financial independence during the period of the ascendancy of the Lords Ordainers and of Lancaster, their powers of coercion would have been very considerably diminished.

Despenser expanded the powers of the Chamber by enabling it to acquire and administer lands and revenues which were exempted from the control of the Exchequer. The King's favourite manor of Langley and the Yorkshire manor of Burstwick-in-Holderness, which he chose as a northern residence, were both administered through the Chamber. Its independence as a state department was further enhanced by the use of its own seal, the *sigillum secretum*.

The final achievement of Despenser was the reorganisation of the 'staple' system which controlled foreign trade.

The staple – the port to which the English exports, wool, wool-fells and hides, were legally compelled to go – had hitherto been a foreign port. Antwerp, Bruges and St Omer had been tried, and each in turn found unsatisfactory. Worsening of Anglo-French relations finally suggested the expedient of basing the staple at home rather than abroad, with safeguards provided for the rights and personal safety of foreign merchants who visited England.

The London merchants would naturally have been best pleased to see the staple based in London, but merchants from other parts of the country were equally eager to argue the advantages of their local ports. It was eventually agreed that the staple should be shared between nine English, three Irish and two Welsh ports, an arrangement which might be expected to be conducive to greater efficiency than that of using a single foreign port. The home-based staple was established by the Kenilworth Ordinance of 1326. It worked well, and was continued in the next reign. Indeed, according to Professor Tout's authoritative statement, 'there was scarcely any detail of staple organisation under Edward III that was not already put into practice under Edward II'.

Despenser may have hoped to strengthen his own position by gaining the support of the influential English merchants with a popular piece of legislation. But by the time the Kenilworth Ordinance was enacted, the train of events which was to lead to the downfall of both Despenser and Edward himself was already far advanced.

The seeds of disaster were sown in the very year of Edward's victory and of Despenser's establishment as his right-hand man. The series of events which led inexorably to their downfall began with one apparently little connected with English affairs: the accession of a new King of France.

In 1322, Charles IV, the third son of Philip IV and the brother

of Isabella, succeeded to the French throne. His accession
impinged upon English affairs only in so far as it necessitated
yet another repetition of Edward's homage for his possessions
in France. It was the autumn of 1323 before King Charles
reminded Edward that his homage was overdue, and invited
him to pay it at Amiens the following Easter. The date of
Edward's going was subsequently altered to July, by which time
an unhappy international complication had arisen.

Despite the conciliatory tone of his letter Charles IV was
following his father's policy of extending his influence over the
English possessions in France. In 1323 he decided to build a
bastide or fortified town at Saint Sardos in the English Agenais.
Saint Sardos itself was technically a French possession, as it was
a priory dependent upon the French Benedictine Abbey at
Sarlat.

161

et desconfortees. Comment
la royne dangleterre ysabel
arriua en angleterre z mes
sire Iehan de haynau. v.e

nsi estoit esmeu
et encouraige mes
sire Iehan de hay
nault et faisoit
la semonce z la priere aux

abbaye par .iij. iours .
Comment la royne dangle
terre assiega le roy son mary
en la ville de bristo. Et est
vj.e Chapitre .

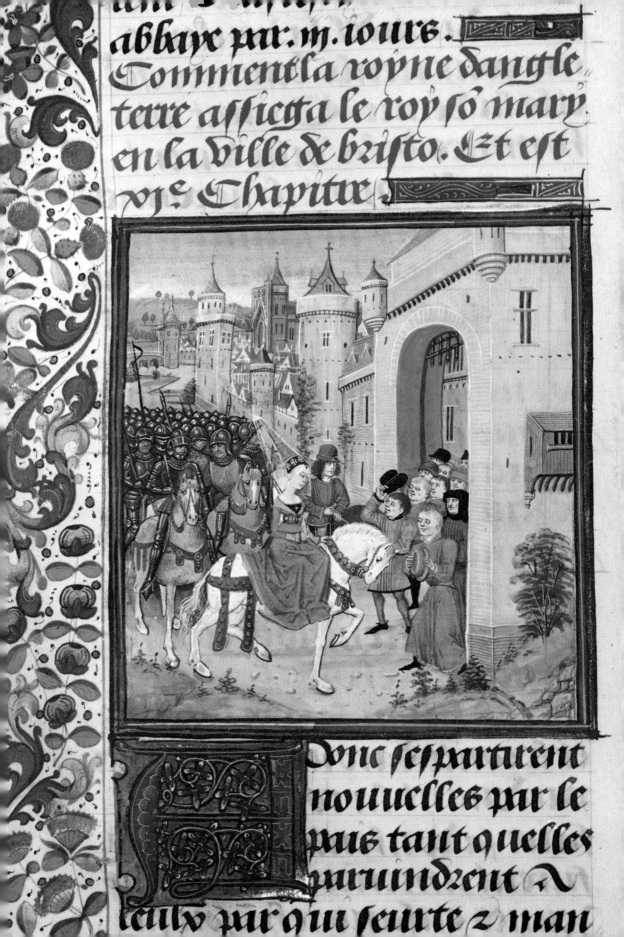

Donc se partirent
nouuelles par le
pais tant quelles
paruindrent a
ceulx par qui seurte z man

Sir Ralph Basset, the English seneschal of Gascony, responded by attacking Saint Sardos in November 1323, and, aided by a local *seigneur*, Bernard de Montpezat, he burned the works which had been begun and hanged a French sergeant on a gallows bearing the arms of France.

Edward II pleaded ignorance of the outrage, and Charles IV accepted his word, but summoned both Basset and Montpezat to appear in his own presence for trial at Toulouse. Both defaulted, and Charles declared that their possessions were forfeit to the French Crown. Edward objected to this judgment and sent the Earl of Kent, a singularly ill-chosen ambassador, to the French Court to discuss the matter. Kent made matters worse by first agreeing to the forfeiture of the castle of Montpezat and then going back on his word. He then made it appear that Edward was not merely delaying his homage to Charles IV while the dispute was unsettled, but refusing it altogether. Charles retaliated by declaring that if this were the case Gascony and Ponthieu were forfeit, and by sending an army under his uncle Charles of Valois to occupy them. Kent fled to the castle of La Réole some thirty miles from Bordeaux, in which Charles of Valois besieged him. In September 1324 Kent made terms, agreeing to a six-month truce.

Kent's ineptitude had caused a frontier incident to escalate into an impending war upon which Edward was most unwilling to enter and for which he was ill-prepared. He appointed a new ambassador to France, one whom he might well have trusted to redeem the situation: Pembroke, the most experienced of peacemakers. Unhappily Pembroke arrived in France only to die leaving his mission unfulfilled. At this point the new Pope, John XXII, intervened. He sent two nuncios to Paris who put forward the suggestion that the person most likely to be able to end the Anglo-French crisis was the wife of one King and the sister of the other, Queen Isabella. Surprisingly, Edward agreed to the proposal.

Earlier in the year, Isabella's estates had been sequestrated on the grounds that hostilities with France were expected and the Queen was a Frenchwoman. Not only was she put on a reduced allowance, but Despenser's wife, Eleanor de Clare, was made her 'housekeeper' and given the right to examine all her correspondence. It looked as though the Queen were little better than a prisoner, and a rumour began to circulate that Despenser was negotiating with the Pope for the annulment of her marriage to Edward. Isabella must have acted with remarkable subtlety and circumspection for Edward and Despenser to have decided that she was sufficiently trustworthy to be allowed to undertake a delicate diplomatic mission to her own country.

That mission provided Isabella with the opportunity for which she had been waiting and the outcome proved that she had prepared herself well. Since 1322 she had been gathering about herself a party of malcontents dedicated to working for the destruction of Hugh Despenser and his father.

At first the Queen's party showed a preponderance of ecclesiastics. Her first and most unscrupulous adherent was Adam Orleton, Bishop of Hereford, who had offended the King by supporting his patron, Lord Mortimer of Wigmore, and the other Marcher rebels in 1321. With him was associated Henry Berghersh, Bishop of Lincoln, an enemy of the King as the nephew of the executed Lord Badlesmere. John Droxford, Bishop of Bath and Wells, was a friend of both of them, and equally inimical to Edward. Indeed, Edward was aware of their enmity if not of their association with the Queen, for in 1322 he had written to the Pope complaining of them, hoping, doubtless, to get them summoned to Avignon, as his father had got the troublesome Archbishop Winchelsey summoned to Rome. John XXII, however, refused to oblige him, and Edward was forced to endure the hated presence of all three prelates.

In the autumn of 1323 Bishop Orleton was instrumental in organising the escape of Mortimer of Wigmore from the Tower. With the aid of liquor and rope provided by two London citizens named Richard de Bettoyne and John de Gisors, Mortimer escaped in classic fashion by making his guards drunk and descending from his prison by the rope. He escaped via Porchester to France where Isabella found him, a ready partisan, when she arrived in Paris.

Other supporters also adhered secretly to her cause, among them John Stratford, Bishop of Winchester, and William Airmyn, Bishop of Norwich. (Both of them had acquired their bishoprics when they had been sent to the Pope to negotiate on behalf of Robert Baldock. In each instance, the Pope had

165

166

Two contrasting views of the fourteenth-century clergy: LEFT A bishop from Wells Cathedral. BELOW An imbibing monk.

apologised to Edward and promised Baldock the next English see to fall vacant. Baldock never obtained his bishopric, for disaster came before preferment.)

The Earl of Kent, fresh from the shame of his unsuccessful embassy, joined Isabella; so did the Earl of Richmond, released by the Scots and offended by the Despensers. Even the King's old friend Sir Henry de Beaumont deserted him, as also did Lancaster's brother the Earl of Leicester, who had aroused the

King's anger by assuming the arms of his late brother without permission and by setting up a cross in his honour at Leicester.

By this time, however, Lancaster's memory had acquired an aura of sanctity unaided by any gesture of fraternal piety. The Despensers were generally hated for their avarice and high-handedness, and Lancaster was remembered as the man who had opposed the régime which they now represented. The fact that Hugh Despenser had sought to adapt and apply what was best in the Ordinances was unrecognised; that Lancaster had upheld the original Ordinances and resisted the King was seized upon as a reason for holding his memory sacred. It was remembered in Lancaster's favour that he had 'worshipped men of religion', and conveniently forgotten that he had 'defouled a great multitude of women and gentle wenches'. An adroit anti-royalist cleric composed a popular liturgy entitled 'The Office of St Thomas of Lancaster', and in due course it was claimed that miracles were taking place at the sites of Lancaster's execution and burial. This unofficial canonisation was, to say the least, a political storm-warning.

Isabella departed for France in March 1325, and by the middle of the summer she had persuaded the King her brother to agree to restore Gascony and Ponthieu to Edward conditionally upon his paying homage for them. The questions of the Agenais and the castle of La Réole were reserved for later discussion, and Isabella remained in Paris awaiting Edward's answer. There can be little doubt that, while she appeared to be negotiating in her husband's interests, Isabella was maturing her own plans, which were greatly expedited by the next series of developments.

Edward now professed his willingness to pay homage for Gascony and Ponthieu, but the Despensers were horrified at the prospect of his leaving England. Their situation, they now recognised, would be alarmingly precarious in his absence. For, if they were still unaware of the secret formation of the Queen's party, they were very well aware of public hatred. Accordingly, they persuaded Edward, whose health had always been robust, to pretend that he was too ill to make the journey to France.

His diplomatic ailment played directly into Isabella's hand. She suggested that their elder son should be permitted to go to France and perform the homage on King Edward's behalf. With what appears from the twentieth-century viewpoint to

Four miniatures from an inferior version of Froissart's Chronicles: Froissart presents a book to Richard II; Isabella is received at Boulogne; Isabella with Prince Edward laying complaints before Charles IV; the siege of Bristol by Isabella's forces.

be the blindest folly, Edward and the Despensers agreed. The thirteen-year-old Prince was created Duke of Aquitaine and Count of Ponthieu and Montreuil, and despatched to France in charge of Bishop Stapledon. On 21 September 1325 he did homage to Charles IV at Vincennes.

The King of France received the homage of his nephew for Gascony and Ponthieu, and then politely informed his brother-in-law that he proposed to retain the Agenais. Edward was enraged. As a means of reasserting the rights which he felt he was better able to defend than his son, to whom he had just surrendered them, he assumed the title of 'Governor and administrator of his first-born, Edward, Duke of Aquitaine, and of his estates'. Charles's answer was to declare all the English territories forfeit once again. The situation was worse than before, and the Duke of Aquitaine had become the pawn of his mother's party and was about to become a helpless participant in the downfall of his father. What he himself knew, at the age of thirteen, of the rights and wrongs of the situation there is no knowing; his future behaviour suggests that the events of the next two years left him the legacy of an uneasy conscience.

It took Bishop Stapledon very little time to assess the situation in France. He found it sufficiently alarming to warrant his leaving the Prince in Paris and returning to England in disguise to report to King Edward. His news was that Isabella had fallen in love with Mortimer of Wigmore, with whom she was living in unconcealed adultery, and that they, together with other English malcontents, were plotting treason, and most probably invasion.

Upon receipt of this alarming news Edward did not lose his nerve. He wrote to the Queen, commanding her to return to England, and his letter was presented jointly to Isabella and her brother the King. Isabella's reply was a public utterance which was at once a plea for sympathy and a refusal to obey her husband:

> I feel that marriage is a joining together of man and woman [she is reported to have said], maintaining the undivided habit of life, and that someone has come between my husband and myself trying to break this bond; I protest that I will not return until this intruder is removed, but, discarding my marriage garment, shall assume the robes of widowhood and mourning until I am avenged.

With these words, or at any rate with a speech to this effect, Isabella declared war on Hugh Despenser. Edward took her ultimatum very seriously. He summoned Parliament, which met on 18 November, and made a speech concerning the Queen's refusal to return, and hinting at his knowledge of Mortimer's influence: 'You know,' he said, '... how providentially as it then seemed, the Queen crossed to France to make peace ... on her departure she did not seem to anyone to be offended. ... But now someone has changed her attitude. Someone has primed her with inventions ... she says that Hugh Despenser is her adversary and hostile to her.' He went on, with astonishing naïvety, 'It is surprising that she has conceived this dislike of Hugh, for when she departed, towards no-one was she more agreeable, myself excepted.'

His words prove, if no other proof were forthcoming, how subtly Isabella had played her hand.

'I firmly believe,' the King concluded, 'that the Queen has been led into this error at the suggestion of someone, and he is in truth wicked and hostile. Now therefore deliberate wisely,

'I will not return until this intruder is removed'

that she ... may be led back to the path of unity by your prudent and kindly reproof.'

It was resolved that a petition, signed by the bishops, should be sent to the Queen, exhorting her to return. Isabella's reply to this and to another firm but reasonable letter from Edward, was an unequivocal refusal. However, her conduct with Mortimer had compromised her in her brother's eyes, for he refused to tolerate her presence any longer. Expelled from France, she made her way to the Court of William II, Count of Hainault, Holland and Zeeland, to whom she proposed a marriage between the Duke of Aquitaine and the Count's daughter Philippa. The Count accepted with alacrity, advanced her a portion of Philippa's dowry to enable her to raise an army for the invasion of England, and lent her the services of his brother John of Hainault, to share with Mortimer the command of her troops.

Throughout 1326 Isabella's invasion was expected, at first from France, and, after her expulsion, from the quarter whence it ultimately came. But the unpopularity of Hugh Despenser made the defence of England very difficult. A fleet was assembled at Portsmouth, but it proved so mutinous that it was quickly disbanded again. Edward and Despenser left the south coast and concentrated their efforts upon organising the defence of London. On 23 September Isabella and her force sailed from Dordrecht, favoured by the winds and unintercepted by English vessels. The following day they entered the Orwell estuary and landed on the coast of Suffolk.

Isabella spent her first night in England at the Earl of Norfolk's castle at Walton-on-the-Naze. Then, appealingly clad in her widow's weeds, she made a pilgrimage to Bury St Edmunds. Local sympathisers flocked to meet her, and many who had supported her secretly now came openly to join her.

In London all was commotion. Edward offered a reward for Mortimer's head, and Archbishop Reynolds issued a papal bull against invaders. It had initially been provided for use against the Scots, but Reynolds hoped that it would be equally appropriate to the present emergency. Unhappily it was greeted with derision. Recently there had been unpleasantness between Reynolds and the King. Reynolds had quarrelled with Archbishop Melton about the latter's right to have his cross carried

Courtly Love

Medieval literature and the vows of knighthood idealised the concept of love, both of men for each other and of men for women. When men or women stepped outside the rules of courtly love, as Edward did in his homosexuality and Isabella in her adultery with Mortimer, they were strongly censured by contemporaries.

LEFT A German writing tablet depicting a hawking party.

ABOVE RIGHT An Italian comb showing dancing couples.
RIGHT Two French ivory mirror cases: a lady crowning her lover and a couple playing chess.

Isabella and her army at Hereford;
in the background is the execution
of Hugh Despenser the Younger.

175

before him in the province of Canterbury, and had been angry when Edward had supported Melton's right, and even angrier when Melton had been appointed Treasurer. Having made his gesture over the papal bull, Reynolds retired to Kent, to see whether the King or the Queen was likely to be victorious before deciding upon further action.

Isabella, accompanied by Mortimer, Norfolk, Henry of Leicester and a rapidly growing army, advanced on London. Edward, occupying the Tower of London, but surrounded by a hostile capital, decided to retire and seek support in the West Country and Wales. He departed, accompanied by the two Despensers, Robert Baldock and the Earls of Arundel and Surrey. London declared for Isabella.

The London mob shed the first blood. An unfortunate man named John the Marshal, a servant of Hugh Despenser and suspected also of being a spy, was executed in the street. The next victim was Bishop Stapledon, who was seized in Cheapside on his way to take sanctuary in St Paul's. He was decapitated with a butcher's knife, and his head was presented to the Queen who received it with a dignified speech of thanks. When order was restored to London, the two citizens who had aided Mortimer's escape in 1324 received their rewards. Richard de Bettoyne became Mayor and John de Gisors was appointed Constable of the Tower.

Meanwhile, the King's party had divided. Edward himself, with Hugh Despenser, went first to Gloucester and thence towards Wales. The Earl of Winchester occupied Bristol. There he encountered the same problem as Edward had experienced in London: the difficulty of holding a castle surrounded by a hostile city.

Isabella advanced on Bristol by way of Oxford, where she paused to hear Bishop Orleton preach a sermon in which, drawing an analogy between the human body and the body politic, he declared that a sick head, which all the remedies of Hippocrates could not heal, were best cut off. This was the first open declaration that Isabella was seeking the severance of the head, not merely the amputation of diseased members. On 26 October she reached Bristol, where the citizens greeted her with enthusiasm, and the Earl of Winchester saw no choice but to surrender.

OPPOSITE Effigy of Philippa of Hainault who married Prince Edward, later Edward III.

177

It is unlikely that Winchester expected mercy, and certainly he did not receive it. On 27 October, Mortimer, Leicester, Norfolk and Kent sat in judgment upon him and sentenced him to death. His end provided an unpleasant contrast with that of Lancaster, which Isabella and her partisans declared themselves to be avenging. Edward's condemnation of Lancaster had been an act of justice, and though he had been a traitor Edward had granted him the relatively decent death of decapitation; Winchester was no traitor, but he was given a traitor's death.

The fall of Bristol reduced Edward to the condition of a hunted fugitive. When Winchester met his end, Edward, Hugh Despenser and Robert Baldock had been at Tintern Abbey. From there they fled to Chepstow and took ship with the intention of sailing to Despenser's island of Lundy, whence they may have hoped to escape to Ireland. But the winds which had aided Isabella's passage to England were not so favourable to Edward's escape. The ship was driven back into Cardiff harbour, the fugitives disembarked again and fled inland, looking for supporters among Despenser's tenants in Glamorgan. It is said that the Welsh nourished an affection for Edward, and certainly Sir Gruffyd Lloyd had been able to raise a Welsh force to fight for him in 1321; in 1326, though he received shelter, sympathy for him was less influential than the unpopularity of Hugh Despenser, whose tenants refused to fight.

While Isabella and Mortimer occupied Hereford, Henry of Leicester and a Welsh cleric named Rhys ap Howel sought for Edward in Glamorgan. On 16 November he was found, some said betrayed, at the Abbey of Neath, where Despenser and Baldock were captured with him. Arundel was captured in Shropshire.

Edward was escorted by Leicester first to Llantrisant and thence to Monmouth, and finally to imprisonment in Kenilworth Castle. Baldock, claiming benefit of clergy, was handed over to Bishop Orleton, who imprisoned him in his London house; subsequently a mob decided that he deserved a worse fate, and dragged him to Newgate where he died. Hugh Despenser was taken to Hereford to meet his end.

On 24 November, he, like his father, was given a semblance of a legal trial. The charges against him included those of

The medieval interior of Tretower Castle in Wales. Edward received shelter in Wales for a few weeks but was eventually captured in Glamorgan.

procuring the execution of the Earl of Lancaster and other barons; of leading the King out of the realm to fight the Scots, and by his own incompetence causing loss and defeat; of advising the King to abandon the Queen at Tynemouth to the peril of her life; of persuading the King to create his father Earl of Winchester and the traitor Harclay Earl of Carlisle; of depriving the Queen of her dower; and of persuading the King to withdraw from the realm, to his great damage and disgrace. What Professor McKisack has called 'this ingenious tissue of fact and fiction' procured the inevitable sentence of death, which was carried out immediately.

Jean Froissart, who described the execution of Hugh Despenser in unsparing detail, reported, 'his member and his testicles were first cut off, because he was a heretic and a sodomite, even, it was said, with the King'. Froissart must have been aware that the English treason sentence always included castration, therefore it must be supposed that its infliction upon the unfortunate Despenser was made the occasion of propaganda designed to lower the King's reputation even further than it had already fallen.

Arundel was also executed, though Surrey was for some unspecified reason permitted to make his peace with the Queen.

With these executions the victory of the She-Wolf of France was complete. It remained only to be seen what fate was in store for the King.

179

6
Edward
the Martyr
1326-7

A royal martyr
even if he were no saint

(John Harvey, *The Plantagenets*)

THE STRENGTH OF KING EDWARD'S POSITION after the battle of Boroughbridge makes the ease with which Isabella achieved his overthrow at first sight astonishing. A variety of causes contributed to her success, not least among them the subtlety with which Isabella had dissembled her hatred of Hugh Despenser and her deepening resentment against her husband, the secrecy with which she had built up her following and the skill with which she had exploited her marital troubles to win herself supporters in Paris, in Hainault and, after her invasion, in England. She had been fortunate in winning the support of the forceful Lord Mortimer and of several astute and unscrupulous bishops, notably Orleton, Berghersh, Stratford and Airmyn. Universal hatred of the Despensers had won her the support of the English magnates, and if lately there had been a thorough elimination of men of ability and ambition from among their ranks, they were nonetheless influential by reason of their great followings, the solid make-weights of the party to which they adhered. If Hugh Despenser had found no rivals among them after Boroughbridge, he found no very willing allies among them when trouble came; they went over to Isabella, with the exception of Arundel and Surrey, who reluctantly supported the King. Surrey, as previously observed, survived Isabella's vengeance; he was permitted to participate in the establishment of the new régime.

Since the flight of the King to Wales, a veneer of legality had been provided for the actions of Isabella's party by the declaration that the young Duke of Aquitaine was Keeper of the Realm during his father's absence, and by the issuing of all commands in his name. Now that the King was a prisoner it was needful to devise a new expedient.

To Isabella and Mortimer the first necessity appeared to be the acquisition of the Great Seal, which was in Edward's possession. Accordingly, on 20 November Bishop Orleton was sent to him at Monmouth to obtain it. That he should be forced to yield the Great Seal to one of his most detested enemies was only the first of Edward's many humiliations; but in this and in most of what followed, he had no choice but to acquiesce and endure.

Isabella received the Great Seal at Hereford, and by its authority issued writs summoning Parliament to meet at

The seal of Edward II.

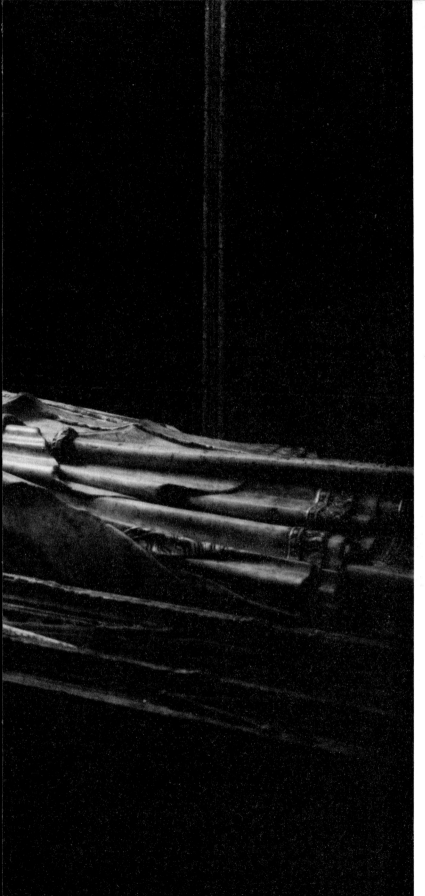

The tomb of Stratford
of Winchester, later
Archbishop of Canterbury,
one of the bishops who
urged Edward to abdicate.

Westminster on 7 January 1327. Although that Parliament was summoned in the King's name, its business was to be his deposition.

Before Parliament met, Edward was visited in his prison at Kenilworth by two of the Queen's bishops, Berghersh of Lincoln and Stratford of Winchester, who formally requested him to appear before Parliament and make a voluntary abdication. According to the Lanercost chronicler, Edward 'utterly refused to comply therewith; nay he cursed them contemptuously, declaring that he would not come among his enemies, or, rather his traitors'. It was evident that his misfortunes had not yet broken his spirit, and the bishops had no choice but to return and inform the Queen and her adherents of the need to proceed without him.

Whether the Westminster Parliament of January 1327 was legally a Parliament, lacking as it did the presence of the King, is arguable. It was, at all events, a very representative assembly of magnates, clergy and commons, and, like the York Parliament of 1322, it included representatives for Wales.

The city, which had been more or less quiet since the violence of the autumn, broke into commotion again, and London mobs rushed to Westminster to force their way into Westminster Hall and add their unruly clamour to the deliberations of those assembled.

The Queen's party made use of propagandist preaching to arouse popular feeling against the King. On 13 January Orleton preached on the text 'A foolish King shall ruin his people', and the crowd, no doubt encouraged by agitators in its midst, responded with shouts of 'We will no more have this man to reign over us.'

'We will no more have this man to reign over us'

The deposition of Edward II was not, however, completely unopposed. Four churchmen bravely spoke up for him: the Archbishop of York, Stephen Gravesend, Bishop of London, Hamo of Hythe, Bishop of Rochester, and Thomas Cobham, Bishop of Worcester. With the exception of Archbishop Melton, they were, in the words of Stubbs, 'pious, learned men but not statesmen'. They were, in any event, supporting a lost cause; but their courage, in the presence of the mobs which had slaughtered Stapledon, was remarkable.

The man whose conduct does least honour to the episcopate

was the King's erstwhile friend Archbishop Reynolds. On 15 January he preached on the text 'The voice of the people is the voice of God', and declared that by the unanimous consent of magnates, clergy and commons, Edward II should be deposed and his eldest son be crowned King in his place. On the same day, it is probable that the Articles of Deposition, the work of Stratford of Winchester, were publicly read.

These articles accused Edward of incompetence to govern, and unwillingness to be guided by the competence of good counsellors; of being controlled by evil counsellors to his own dishonour, and of giving himself up to unseemly works and occupations; of losing Scotland and many territories in Gascony and Ireland left him by his father, and of losing the friendship of the King of France; of persecuting churchmen (Orleton, Berghersh and Droxford, presumably) and of putting to death, exiling, imprisoning and disinheriting many great men; of violating his coronation oath, which bound him to do justice to all, and of showing himself incorrigible in all these doings, beyond hope of amendment. Stratford's Articles of Deposition could be described, like the indictment of Hugh Despenser, as an 'ingenious tissue of fact and fiction'.

On 16 January a deputation was sent by Parliament to the King at Kenilworth to bring him the news of his deposition. The deputation consisted of two earls, Henry of Leicester and the traitorous but fortunate Surrey; three bishops, Orleton, Stratford, and probably another false friend, Hotham of Ely; four barons and four knights; an abbot, a prior and four friars; three citizens of London and two representatives for the Cinque Ports; and two or three commons to represent the other towns of England. The spokesman for the deputation was Sir William Trussell, a knight formerly in the service of Thomas of Lancaster, who had pronounced the sentence of death upon Hugh Despenser.

Even at this late stage of the proceedings Edward was urged to make a voluntary abdication: the greater appearance of legality the new régime could achieve, the more secure it would be. Orleton and Stratford saw the King before the rest of the deputation was admitted to his presence, and they attempted to win his compliance by persuasion. When the King refused, Orleton resorted to threats and told him that if he would not abdicate willingly, the people of England would repudiate not only him but also his son, and would set up a King who was not of the blood royal. Successfully blackmailed by the threatened extinction of his dynasty, and presumably by the threatened usurpation of Mortimer, the King broke down and agreed to abdicate in favour of his son. Whether, even at this moment, Mortimer possessed power sufficient to permit of usurpation may be doubted; he was not independent of the Queen, who, infatuated with him as she was, must have had the future of her son at heart. To Edward II, however, the threat seemed sufficiently real.

His abdication was a dramatic scene. Edward, clad in a black gown, received the full deputation, and, before a word was spoken, fell down in a dead faint. Orleton, whose brutality had reduced him to such a pitiable condition, raised him and reiterated the demand that the King should voluntarily abdicate. With copious tears Edward answered that while he grieved that his people had repudiated him, he rejoiced that they were content to crown his son. Sir William Trussell, declaring that he spoke on behalf of the whole kingdom, then renounced all homage and allegiance to King Edward; and Sir Thomas Blount, the Steward of the Household, broke his staff to signify that the King's Household was disbanded. The reign of Edward II was over; he was henceforth to be known as 'the Lord Edward, sometime King of England'.

Edward III was crowned by Archbishop Reynolds on 1 February 1327. His father remained in the custody of Henry of Leicester, who was permitted to assume the title of his dead brother Lancaster.

The new Earl of Lancaster is said to have treated his royal prisoner with respect, and to have permitted him to live at least in comfort if not in state. It was while Edward remained in Lancaster's custody at Kenilworth Castle that he may have written the Anglo-Norman poem on the subject of his downfall and imprisonment which has been fairly convincingly attributed to him. The poem has been described as 'a rare and valuable specimen of Anglo-Norman lyric poetry'. The first verse serves both as a sample of the King's verse-making and as a very fair epitaph on his reign:

Edwardus iij
p' conquestu

Anno dñi mⁱ CCC xxxᵛⁱ...
Regnavit filius coronatus Edwardus...
regni sui quinto...

After him regned his sone ful vigist
þe pridde Edward þat doughti kyng.
þre Sonys he hadd truli here,
þat to him were bothe lefe & dere.
ffirst þe kyngs did a grete maistrey.
Atte Sluce he breuned a grete flete.
Atte Cresse ic fraught here a gayn.
The kyng of Beme þer was slaine.
And þe kyng of ffrance put to flight.
No lenger þan durst he fight.

A Sege at Calice he les bifore.
þat lestid wele mounthe and more.
And as he þens wuld go.
he wanne Calice and townis mo.
At þe bataille of Peytois, bi ordenaunce
was tak þe kyng off ffrance.
At Westmestre he lieth here.
he regnid alle most li yere.
As for him dede prince Edward
which had a sone þat hete Richard.

En temps de iver me survynt damage,
Fortune trop m'ad traversé:
Eure m'est faili tut mon age:
Bient sovent le ay esprové:
En mond n'ad si bel ne si sage,
Ne si curtois ne si preysé,
Si eur ne lui court de avantage,
Que il ne serra pur fol clamé.

It has been literally translated as follows:

In winter woe befell me;
By cruel Fortune thwarted,
My life now lies a ruin.
Full oft have I experienced,
There's none so fair, so wise,
So courteous nor so highly famed,
But, if Fortune cease to favour,
Will be a fool proclaimed.

If Edward wrote the poem at Kenilworth he would have written it between November 1326 and April 1327. On 3 April Edward was taken from the custody of the scrupulous, even gentle Henry of Lancaster, and put into the hands of two less kindly gaolers.

Edward's new custodians were Thomas de Berkeley and Sir John Maltravers. Thomas de Berkeley had been captured with his father, Sir Maurice de Berkeley, at Boroughbridge. Sir Maurice had died in prison and his estates had been given to Hugh Despenser. Thomas owed his liberation and the restoration of his inheritance to Queen Isabella. He had little reason to have kindly feelings towards Edward, and his commitment to the new régime had recently been strengthened by his marriage to Mortimer's daughter. Sir John Maltravers was Thomas de Berkeley's brother-in-law, a fugitive from Boroughbridge who had joined Isabella's party in France.

The transferring of Edward from the custody of Henry of Lancaster to that of these two avowed enemies was the sinister prelude to the last phase of his life. From Kenilworth Castle he was taken to Llantony Abbey in Monmouthshire, where he spent the night of Palm Sunday, 4 April. The following day he completed his journey to Berkeley Castle. From then onwards, what happened to him no longer happened before the public

The courtyard and keep of Berkeley Castle, where Edward was taken to be murdered.

eye; plenty of gossip came out of Berkeley, but few facts.

His disappearance and death were almost essential to the survival of the new régime. Once the Despensers had been done away with, the sympathy which Isabella had contrived to inspire naturally declined; it sank to nothing when her partisans had the opportunity to examine the situation at leisure. The Queen had played the part of a much-wronged wife with consummate skill; but the truth was that she was an adulteress whose partisans had fought for her only to discover that they had fought to establish the authority of her lover Mortimer. And, since Mortimer was quite as arrogant and avaricious as Hugh Despenser, it soon became obvious that the situation at the centre of English political life was no whit better than before. The new King, unscrupulously manipulated by his mother and Mortimer, was still too young to be able to assert his own authority. It was small wonder that there was a wave of public sympathy for the deposed Edward, and small wonder that the sympathy was strong enough to show itself in conspiracies to secure his release.

Research carried out earlier in this century revealed that one of these conspiracies, led by the brothers Dunheved, was briefly successful. Stephen Dunheved, lord of the manor of Dunchurch, near Rugby, was a supposedly banished man who maintained himself as the leader of a band of outlaws. Dunheved was the reality of the type represented by the legendary Robin Hood: a brutal robber, a perpetrator of savage homicides, but a man who was capable of organising an operation as ambitious as breaking into a great castle and rescuing a King. Thomas Dunheved was a Dominican friar, said by the Lanercost chronicler to have been the emissary sent to Avignon by Hugh Despenser to negotiate the annulment of the marriage of Edward and Isabella. He, in all probability, would have been the initiator of the attempted rescue.

Sometime in July, the outlaws attacked Berkeley Castle, forced an entry and looted the castle, 'ravished the father of the King out of the hands of the guard' and made off with him, possibly to Corfe in Dorset. However, Edward was swiftly recaptured and taken back to his prison. Thomas Dunheved, taken with him, appears to have met his end in Berkeley Castle. Stephen the outlaw escaped.

At the time the King's escape and recapture were not publicised, but the chronicler Adam Murimuth, who wrote some eighteen years later, had evidently heard something about it, for he wrote: ' … because they were afraid of certain persons coming to him to effect his release, Edward was secretly removed from Berkeley by night, and taken to Corfe and other secret places, but at last they took him back to Berkeley, but after such a fashion that it could hardly be ascertained where he was'.

This was perhaps the nucleus of the story, later elaborated by a more sensational writer, Geoffrey le Baker, of how Edward had been dragged around the countryside by night and subjected to numerous indignities, such as being crowned with a crown of hay and shaved with ditchwater. It is of course quite likely that Edward's rescuers had urged him to shave his beard to avoid recognition, and that ditch-water was the only water available for the purpose. The rest is probably fictitious hagiography, for it was written when Edward, like Thomas of Lancaster, had received an unofficial canonisation, inspired by popular sympathy for his fate.

That fate was inevitably hastened by the so nearly successful rescue, and sealed when another conspiracy to free him was discovered. The second projected rescue, planned by a Welsh knight named Sir Rhys ap Grufydd, was betrayed to Mortimer, who was now Justice of Wales, by his lieutenant, William of Shalford. Mortimer, who was at Abergavenny, received Shalford's information on 7 September. From Abergavenny he sent to Berkeley a man named William Ogle who was instructed to deliver Shalford's letter to Sir John Maltravers and to Sir Thomas Gurney who, under Thomas de Berkeley, now shared the charge of Edward's safekeeping. Berkeley, it appears, understood that his part was to remain in ignorance of what

Corfe Castle, where Edward may have briefly regained his liberty after a rescue attempt.

193

Eating and drinking were very much a
feature of medieval life and it was on public
occasions such as feasts (ABOVE) that Edward,
absorbed in his favourites, had aroused the enmity
of the barons and the Queen.
RIGHT   A contemporary face jug of Edward II.
OPPOSITE   A cellarer passes drinking flasks to the
customers in the tavern scene from a treatise on the
seven deadly sins.

194

A fourteenth-century bronze ewer, believed to come from Berkeley Castle.

was done to his prisoner; Maltravers, Gurney and Ogle were to take responsibility for it. All this secret activity was followed on 21 September by an official announcement that the father of the King was dead.

The contemporary St Paul's annalist reported merely that Edward had died at Berkeley; but before long other stories were in circulation. Murimuth, the chronicler who had heard something about the Dunheved conspiracy, had likewise heard something about Edward's death. He wrote: 'Many persons, abbots, priors, knights, burgesses of Bristol and Gloucester, were summoned to view his body, and indeed superficially examined it, nevertheless it was commonly said that he was

196

slain as a precaution by the orders of Sir John Maltravers and Sir Thomas Gurney.'

Before many years had passed, Ranulph Higden, author of the Latin *Polychronicon*, recounted the terrible manner in which Edward was said to have met his end: '*Cum veru ignito inter celanda confossus ignominiose peremptus est*', i.e., 'He was ignominiously slain with a red-hot spit thrust into the anus.' It was a death which would have served the double purpose of being a savage act of poetic justice upon the form of pleasure which Edward was believed to have enjoyed, and a way of killing him which would have left the body unmarked when it was laid out in seemly fashion before the gaze of the abbots, priors, knights and burgesses of Bristol and Gloucester. Higden's story carries a certain amount of conviction because his first translator was John Trevisa, who became vicar of Berkeley not many years after Edward's death, and he, who would have known what was locally believed concerning it, translated Higden's statement without comment.

At the time of Edward's death the attention of the government was engaged elsewhere, for the truce with Scotland had been prematurely broken, and Edward III had been taken by Mortimer on his first Scottish campaign. It was as inglorious and inconclusive as any of the campaigns undertaken by his father, a very muted beginning to the career of one of the most militaristic of English kings.

The body of Edward II was embalmed, and his heart, encased in a silver casket, was sent by Thomas de Berkeley to Isabella, who received it with hypocritical sorrow. Hypocrisy was the keynote of the lavish funeral which took place at Gloucester in December, and was attended by Isabella, clad once more in widow's weeds.

The body of the King was borne through the streets of Gloucester on a hearse drawn by horses whose harness was emblazoned with the leopards of the royal arms of England. The hearse itself was supported on the backs of carved lions, and ornamented with images of the four evangelists and of angels bearing golden censers. The whole was covered in gold leaf. On top of the coffin lay a painted effigy of the King, crowned with a copper-gilt crown. Solid oaken barriers had been set up to hold back the crowds which filled the streets to watch the royal funeral. Popular interest and emotion, it seems, were very great; soon after Edward's burial pilgrims began to visit the tomb in the Abbey Church of St Peter to venerate the dead King as a saint and martyr. At his tomb, as at the tomb of Thomas of Lancaster, it was soon claimed that miracles were performed.

Edward III, troubled in conscience at the part which he had been made to play in his father's downfall, did not yet feel that sufficient honours had been paid him by way of reparation. However, a few more years passed before he was able to rid himself of Mortimer's influence and be free to rule and to follow the dictates of his conscience in this matter.

It was perhaps fortunate for Edward III's subsequent reputation that he himself was not responsible for the 'disgraceful peace' signed with Scotland in 1328; to Mortimer fell the unpopularity and the loss of prestige reserved for those who are forced to come to terms with the inevitable. By the Treaty of Northampton, the full sovereignty of the King of Scots was at last recognised, and Edward III's young sister Joan of the Tower was married to King Robert's son David, who in 1329 became King David II.

The following year Edward III organised the *coup d'état* which overthrew Mortimer. In October 1330, Mortimer was arrested at Nottingham Castle and taken to London, where, a few weeks later, he suffered a traitor's death. Though Edward III ignored his mother's desperate plea 'Fair son, have pity on the gentle Mortimer', he treated Isabella herself with a politic blend of sternness and generosity. She was banished from Court, and though she was not imprisoned, her movements were discreetly controlled; but she was granted an allowance of £3,000 a year and permitted to live in comfort as a private person. She lived for the most part at Castle Rising in Norfolk, and occupied herself with good works. She died in 1358, and was buried in the habit of the Franciscan order of the Poor Clares. She took with her to her grave in the Franciscan church at Newgate the secret of whether she had or had not any connection with the murder of the King her husband.

Apart from Mortimer, who paid the full penalty for all his treasons, those who had been connected with Edward II's death were never brought to justice. Thomas de Berkeley, indeed,

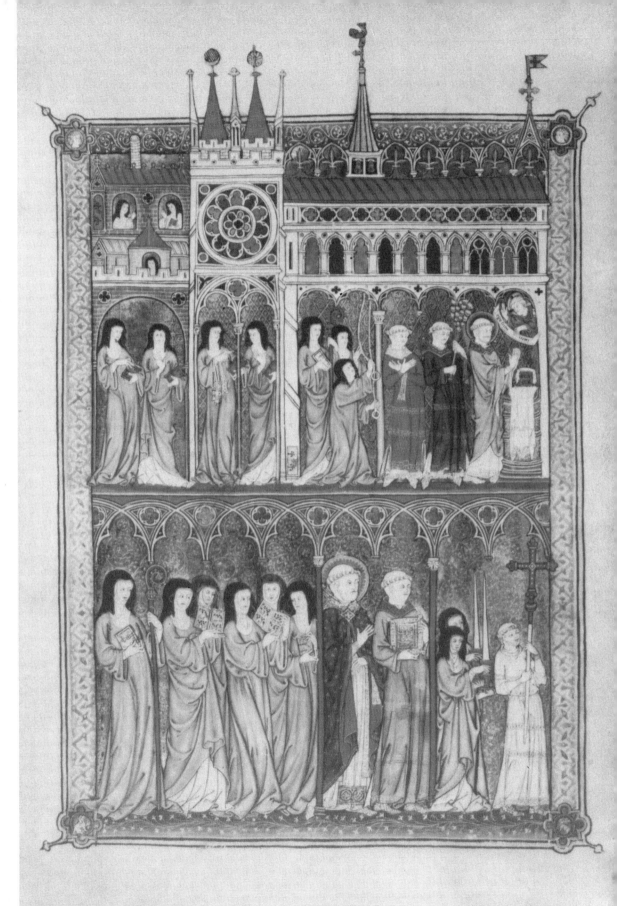

was prosecuted, but his plea of ignorance was ultimately accepted. Ogle was arrested, but escaped to die a free man. Gurney was arrested twice; the first time he escaped, and the second time died in the hands of his captors. Maltravers found it prudent to live abroad, but he did good service to Edward III in Flanders, and received a full pardon before his death in 1364. Clearly the King preferred that while there should be a public appearance of an attempt to see justice done, the truth concerning his father's fate should not be permitted to come to light. Perhaps this was the only possible way of protecting what remained of Queen Isabella's good name.

The reparation which Edward III offered his father was to build for him a magnificent memorial. It survives to the present day, in the church which is now Gloucester Cathedral. It consists of an intricate and delicate double canopy of limestone and purbeck marble, raised above the tomb upon which lies an alabaster effigy of the King, a masterpiece of English medieval carving, deliberately conceived as an image of saintly majesty.

The cult of Edward II was encouraged by the piety of his son, who visited the tomb as a pilgrim, and by the example of other royal pilgrims, Edward III's Queen, Philippa of Hainault, his son the Black Prince, and his sister Joan, Queen of Scots. Later in the century the murdered King's great-grandson, Richard II, made strenuous but unavailing efforts to secure his formal canonisation. However, the cult was maintained not merely by the piety of the royal family, it was popular and spontaneous, and it endured until the end of the fifteenth century, probably until the eve of the Reformation, when the veneration of all local saints, official and unofficial, declined and at last ceased. But for almost two centuries Edward II, like Thomas of Lancaster, was an unofficial saint; and, human nature being an inconsistent thing, no doubt there were many people who made pilgrimages to both Pontefract and Gloucester.

Edward II was perhaps almost as undeserving of canonisation as Thomas of Lancaster; but if both of them lacked the heroic virtues of sanctity, it can at least be said for Edward that he was the more amiable personality. He possessed, indeed, some agreeable traits of character, and some good qualities which are deserving of respect. It can be truly said of him that he was a

200

Decorated Gothic

The first half of the fourteenth century
was one of the most brilliant periods of
English architecture, when the ever-
increasing wealth of the Church
provided the means for continual
rebuilding and beautifying. The finest
Decorated cathedral is Exeter, which,
apart from the Norman towers, was
rebuilt to a uniform design by
successive bishops. Although the nave
(far right) was not built until the
1330s, the design follows so closely that
of the choir and presbytery (1288–1309)
that the spirit of the whole is early
fourteenth century.

RIGHT The ceiling of the chapter house
at Wells Cathedral.
BELOW The view looking up into the
octagon at Ely, a unique achievement
of the late Decorated period.

man 'who loved not wisely but too well'; yet the fidelity of his affections was in itself not discreditable. Nor is it discreditable to him that those whom he loved showed a reciprocal fidelity. When Edward was Prince of Wales Gaveston was described by way of criticism, as 'loving the King's son inordinately'. Both Gaveston and Despenser, though they were too much hated by Edward's enemies for it to have been possible for them to recoup their fortunes by betraying him, might have re-made their careers by fleeing abroad and seeking service with some foreign potentate. Both of them chose to remain with Edward and endure the consequences of their fidelity.

Edward did not enjoy the loyalty only of his favourites, he was loyally served by some of the most respected men of the age: Archbishop Melton, and Bishops Stapledon, Gravesend, Hythe and Cobham. He retained the affection of his sisters and of his step-mother, Margaret of France, and the friendship of the most respected of the magnates, Aymer de Valence, Earl of Pembroke.

If Edward failed to win the love and respect of his subjects in general, it was said by a chronicler writing in the next reign 'When ... all England would rid herself of him, then the Welsh in a wonderful manner cherished and esteemed him, and, as far as they were able, stood by him grieving over his adversities both in life and in his death, and composing mournful songs about him in the language of their country.'

He was a man who possessed two qualities which are generally appreciated by the English: physical courage and a sense of humour. Furthermore, he was usually just, and not, by the standards of his times, unusually severe, even when justice demanded the meting out of punishments. Those who died a traitor's death in his reign were traitors, and when he obtained his long-desired revenge upon Thomas of Lancaster he was by no means vindictive. His moderation contrasts creditably with the vindictiveness of Isabella.

For the rest, there is plenty of evidence of his generosity to his servants, and of his friendliness and informality towards ordinary people. If his liking for informal pleasures shocked his contemporaries, it seems shocking no longer; indeed, it provides an agreeable sidelight on his tragic career.

Even though Edward II failed as a King, it is impossible to

Edward

LEFT Two figures said to
represent Edward and
Isabella from Walter de
Milemete's treatise of 1326,
which was presented
to Edward III.

RIGHT Edward II from a
*Chronicle of the Kings
of England*.

avoid the impression that he was unfortunate far beyond his deserts. He had had the difficult inheritance of succeeding an almost legendary father, and of becoming responsible for his father's uncompleted conquests, foreign entanglements and unpaid debts. Contemporary chroniclers and later historians are almost unanimous in their verdict that his reign was disastrous; yet it is possible to argue that during his later years success and disaster hung in the balance. Edward's most recent biographer, Mr Harold F. Hutchison, has written a convincing account of how near he came to consolidating the success of Boroughbridge. Certainly, in the brief period of success which followed his victory, Edward deserves the credit for appointing intelligent and able ministers in the Despensers, Stapledon, Melton and Baldock. Perhaps the denouement of the reign should be blamed not upon the incompetence of Edward but upon the hubris of Despenser, which led him into the fatal folly of antagonising the Queen.

As far as the character of Edward's reign is concerned, a near-contemporary stated simply, 'The commonalty under Edward were not oppressed.' Professor Tout wrote more explanatorily, 'the people were much better off than under the glorious rule of his father. There was far less taxation, no extortions ... far less conscription, no foreign service, no winter campaigns in Scotland.' Apart from the famine years of 1315 and 1316, and always excepting the miserable condition of the Border counties, Edward's reign showed a modest but increasing prosperity.

Despite the marchings and counter-marchings of royalist and Lancastrian forces, despite the invasion of Isabella and the tragic conclusion of the reign, life in England continued for the most part relatively undisturbed. God was worshipped and the land cultivated. Even the least privileged section of the population, manorial tenants who were bound to the land, had fifty-two Sundays and fifty-six holy days on which they were free to enjoy themselves. Men and women who had freedom of movement and sufficient money combined piety and pleasure by going on pilgrimages. Men who quarrelled with their neighbours brought their disputes before the courts quite as frequently as they resorted to violence. Men like Stephen Dunheved committed acts of violence sometimes on a large

'The commonalty under Edward were not oppressed'

scale, but often they were successfully brought to justice and punished with a severity intended to deter others who might be tempted to do likewise.

The troubles of the reign did not deter those who desired to secure their own immortality, or to display their piety, from financing learned and ecclesiastical foundations. In 1318 Edward II's government secured from Pope John XXII the bull which formalised the foundation of the University of Cambridge; and in 1312 a bull had been obtained for the foundation of a shortlived University of Dublin. Edward II himself provided at Oxford a habitation for the Carmelite Friars, and at Cambridge founded a King's Hall for the children of the Chapel Royal. At Oxford, the unfortunate Bishop Stapledon founded Exeter College, and a chancery clerk named Adam of Brome founded Oriel. Pious ladies were not to be outdone. Roger Damory's widow, Elizabeth de Clare, was the foundress of Clare College, while Pembroke College was founded by Marie de St Pol, the widow of Aymer de Valence.

The increasing prosperity of English merchants found a different form of expression. At the beginning of the reign, Edward II had sought financial assistance from the Frescobaldi, who fell with Gaveston, and at the end of the reign, he had had some assistance from the Bardi, who likewise fell with Despenser. But Despenser's legislation concerning the Staple ports may well have assisted the increasing prosperity of English merchant families. It was not foreign banking houses like the Frescobaldi, Bardi and Peruzzi who financed Edward III, but the newly established English houses of Pole and Conduit, the foundations of whose fortunes were laid in the reign of Edward II.

In the arts, the period was by no means undistinguished. It saw the development of the decorated style in Gothic architecture. Here again the name of Bishop Stapledon recurs, as the man whose patronage produced the magnificent nave of Exeter Cathedral. Building done in the reign of Edward II survives at York, Tewkesbury and Ely. York and Tewkesbury possess examples of the stained glass of the period, some of which is very beautiful, though it is generally considered inferior to the stained glass of the previous century. Little early-fourteenth-

Rural Life

Edward II's reign showed a modest but increasing prosperity. God was worshipped and the land cultivated despite the political turmoils of the reign. Even the least privileged members of the population had fifty-two Sundays and fifty-six holy days on which they were free to enjoy themselves.

BELOW and RIGHT Two common rural occupations, scything and sheep keeping. BELOW RIGHT Women making garlands of flowers.

century painting survives, but there was a flourishing East-Anglian school of illuminators, whose very existence is illustrative of the fact that it is possible to over-stress the disorder of the period.

In literature, verse romances were the most popular reading matter of royalty and nobility, and of such knights as were literate. Queen Isabella herself possessed eight romances, among them 'a great book covered in white leather concerning the deeds of Arthur', and the romance of *Aimeri of Narbonne*. Perhaps the most interesting literary development of the reign was the appearance of an immensely long poem, *Cursor Mundi*, which in spite of its title was written in the northern dialect of English. It is a work of religious history, enormous in scope and running to some thirty thousand lines. It possesses considerable interest both as an early example of the use of English as a literary language, and as the source from which the authors of the York cycle of mystery plays, dating from the next reign, derived their material.

A single example of dramatic writing survives from the reign of Edward II, a fragment of a comedy entitled the *Clerk and Damsel*. It is fitting that one of the earliest surviving examples of drama should belong to Edward's reign, since he himself is recorded as having been an enthusiastic patron of plays and players. Indeed, it was maliciously said that Archbishop Reynolds initially owed his preferment to his talents as a producer and director rather than to any more relevant qualifications.

All in all, despite political troubles and ultimate failure, it may be said that the reign of Edward II, though inglorious, was not altogether discreditable.

It was a reign to which there was a curious epilogue. It takes the form of an undated letter written by a Genoese priest named Manuel Fieschi, who held an English benefice, to King Edward III. Fieschi recounted that he had received in confession from King Edward II himself the story of how he had escaped from Berkeley Castle. The first part of the letter gives an absolutely accurate account of all that befell Edward from his flight to Chepstow to his imprisonment at Berkeley. Then follows the story that a servant at Berkeley told Edward that Sir Thomas Gurney and one Simon Barford were going to kill

OPPOSITE A king oversees his builders, from a fourteenth-century romance.

212

him. The servant offered to change clothes with Edward so that he might escape in disguise. Edward accepted, and thus disguised reached the gate of the castle where he found the porter asleep. Edward slew him, took his keys, and made his escape in safety. Gurney and Barford, fearing the anger of the Queen if Edward's escape were discovered, presented the porter's body on public view as that of the King, and sent the heart to the Queen. The porter's body was duly buried with all the solemnities described, at Gloucester.

Meanwhile, said Fieschi, Edward had taken refuge first at Corfe Castle, and from there had made his way to Ireland. Subsequently he returned to England and went thence to France, Flanders and finally Languedoc. At Avignon he was received in audience by Pope John XXII, to whom he revealed his identity, and who entertained him honourably and in secrecy for fifteen days. Ultimately he made his way to northern Italy, where he became a hermit, and lived a life of prayer and penance for his own sins and those of others. It appeared that he was still alive at the time of writing.

The story is full of difficulties and improbabilities, chiefly that it presupposes an extraordinarily strong likeness between Edward II and the porter of Berkeley Castle. Nonetheless, even if such a likeness did not exist, the resulting problem might not have been insuperable. We do not know how long the King had been dead when the announcement of his death was made, or how long after the announcement the body was publicly displayed. It might not have been too readily recognisable by the time the people mentioned by Murimuth 'superficially examined it'. When Isabella saw it, if indeed she looked within the coffin, it was already embalmed.

According to Professor Tout, Fieschi's letter 'is a remarkable document, so specious and detailed, and bearing none of those marks by which the gross medieval forgery can generally be detected'. 'Yet,' he wrote, 'who can believe it true? ... Was it simply a fairy tale? Was it the real confession of a madman?' – the victim of a delusion, like John of Powderham – '... Or was it an intelligent attempt to exact hush money from a famous King whose beginnings had been based upon his father's murder and his mother's adultery?' Perhaps the last suggestion is the most likely.

OPPOSITE A king, possibly Edward II, from the west door of Lincoln Cathedral.

215

However, throughout history myths of survival have gathered around heroes and around men who have met their deaths mysteriously. Popular heroes as diverse as King Arthur, James IV of Scotland, Lord Kitchener and Lawrence of Arabia have inspired myths of survival and impending return. Edward II, Richard II, the Princes in the Tower and the last Tsar of Russia and his family inspired survival myths not because popular admiration expressed itself in reluctance to accept the fact of their deaths, but because a part of the human mind wishes to deny the fact of iniquitous and secret murder, and to seek a happier explanation of disappearance. Furthermore, in the majority of the instances mentioned, a political purpose could be served by the rumour that the victims were still alive.

While it is not absolutely beyond the bounds of possibility that Edward II could have escaped from his prison to end his life as a hermit, far more probably the unhappy truth is that he expiated his sins and follies and paid the penalty of failure with a terrible end in the dungeons of Berkeley Castle.

OPPOSITE The wheel of fortune from the Holkham Bible picture book. This dates from the mid-fourteenth century and is possibly a comment on the fall of Edward II. The king's four sayings are: '*regnabo, regno, regnavi; sum sine regno*'.

Select bibliography

Barbour, John, *The Bruce*, trans. and ed. Archibald A. H. Douglas (Glasgow, 1964)

Barrow, G. W. S., *Robert Bruce and the Community of the Realm of Scotland* (London, 1965)

Edwards, Kathleen, *The Political Importance of the English Bishops during the Reign of Edward II* (*English Historical Review*, Vol. LIX Jan.–Sept. 1944)

Froissart, *Chronicles*, ed. Geoffrey Brereton (Penguin Classics, 1968)

Grassi, J. L., *William Airmyn and the Bishopric of Norwich* (*English Historical Review*, Vol. LXX Jan.–Oct. 1955)

Halliday, F. E., *An Illustrated Cultural History of England* (London, 1967)

Harvey, John, *The Plantagenets* (London, 1948)

Higden (see *Polychronicon*)

Holmes, G. A., *Judgement on the Younger Despenser, 1326* (*English Historical Review*, Vol. LXX Jan.–Oct. 1955)

Hutchison, Harold F., *Edward II: The Pliant King* (London, 1971)

Johnstone, Hilda, *The Eccentricities of Edward II* (*English Historical Review*, Vol. XLVIII, Jan.–Oct. 1933)

Johnstone, Hilda, *Edward of Carnarvon, 1284–1307* (Manchester University Press, 1946)

Johnstone, Hilda, *Isabella, the She-Wolf of France* (*History*. New Series, Vol. XXI, June 1936–March 1937)

Maddicott, J. R., *Thomas of Lancaster, 1307–1322: a Study in the Reign of Edward II* (Oxford University Press, 1970)

Maxwell, Sir Herbert, ed., *The Chronicle of Lanercost, 1272–1346* (Glasgow, 1913)

McKisack, May, *The Fourteenth Century, 1307–1399* (Oxford, 1959)

Polychronicon Ranulphi Higden, Monachi Cestrensis, together with the English translations of John Trevisa and of an unknown writer of the Fifteenth Century. ed. Joseph Rawson Lumby (Rolls Series, London 1882)

Stubbs, William, ed. *Chronicles of the Reigns of Edward I and Edward II.* 2 vols. (London, 1882, 1883)

Studer, Paul, *An Anglo-Norman Poem by Edward II, King of England*

(*Modern Language Review*, Vol. XVI, Jan.–Oct. 1921)

Tanquerey, Frédéric J., *The Conspiracy of Thomas Dunheved, 1327* (*English Historical Review*, Vol. XXXI, Jan.–Oct. 1916)

Tout, T. F., *The Captivity and Death of Edward of Carnarvon* (Reprint from the *Bulletin of the John Rylands Library*. Manchester University Press, 1920)

Tout, T. F., *The History of England from the Accession of Henry III to the Death of Edward III, 1216–1377* (*The Political History of England in Twelve Volumes*, Vol. III, London 1905)

Tout, T. F., *The Place of the Reign of Edward II in English History* (Manchester University Press, 1914)

Vickers, Kenneth H., *England in the Later Middle Ages* (7th ed. London, 1950)

Vita Edwardi Secundi, Monachi Cuiusdam Malmsberiensis (The Life of Edward the Second by the So-Called Monk of Malmesbury) trans. and ed. N. Denholm-Young (London, 1957)

Wright, Thomas, ed. *The Political Songs of England, from the Reign of John to that of Edward II* (Camden Society, 1839)

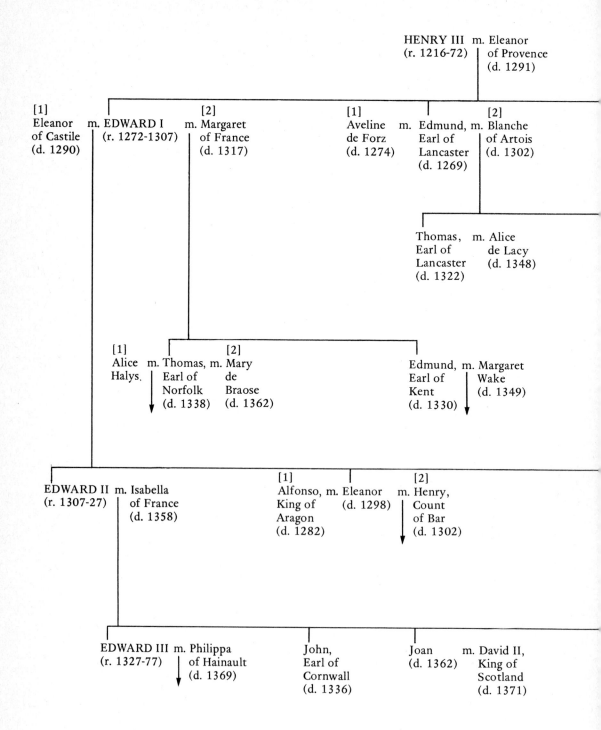

HENRY III m. Eleanor
(r. 1216-72) | of Provence
(d. 1291)

[1]
Eleanor m. EDWARD I
of Castile (r. 1272-1307)
(d. 1290)

[2]
m. Margaret
of France
(d. 1317)

[1]
Aveline m. Edmund, m. Blanche
de Forz Earl of of Artois
(d. 1274) Lancaster (d. 1302)
(d. 1269)

[2]

Thomas, m. Alice
Earl of de Lacy
Lancaster (d. 1348)
(d. 1322)

[1]
Alice m. Thomas, m. Mary
Halys. Earl of de
Norfolk Braose
(d. 1338) (d. 1362)

[2]

Edmund, m. Margaret
Earl of Wake
Kent (d. 1349)
(d. 1330)

EDWARD II m. Isabella
(r. 1307-27) of France
(d. 1358)

[1]
Alfonso, m. Eleanor
King of (d. 1298)
Aragon
(d. 1282)

[2]
m. Henry,
Count
of Bar
(d. 1302)

EDWARD III m. Philippa
(r. 1327-77) of Hainault
(d. 1369)

John,
Earl of
Cornwall
(d. 1336)

Joan m. David II,
(d. 1362) King of
Scotland
(d. 1371)

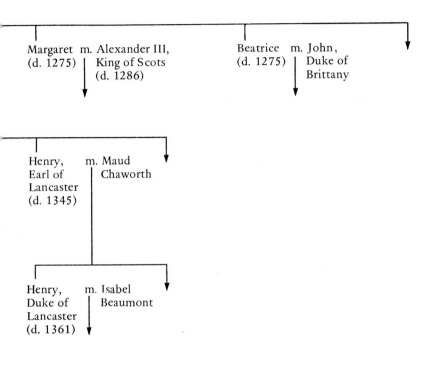

Margaret m. Alexander III,
(d. 1275) | King of Scots
          (d. 1286)

Beatrice m. John,
(d. 1275) | Duke of
           Brittany

Henry, m. Maud
Earl of   Chaworth
Lancaster
(d. 1345)

Henry, m. Isabel
Duke of   Beaumont
Lancaster
(d. 1361)

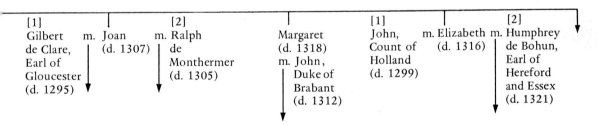

[1]
Gilbert   m. Joan   m. Ralph
de Clare,   (d. 1307) | de
Earl of   Monthermer
Gloucester   (d. 1305)
(d. 1295)

[2]

Margaret
(d. 1318)
m. John,
| Duke of
  Brabant
  (d. 1312)

[1]
John,   m. Elizabeth m. Humphrey
Count of   (d. 1316) | de Bohun,
Holland   Earl of
(d. 1299)   Hereford
                         and Essex
                         (d. 1321)

[2]

Eleanor   m. Reginald,
(d. 1355) | Duke of
            Guelders
            (d. 1343)

Index